About the Author

Edwin Ossa was born in Jackson Heights Queens, New York, Edwin Antonio Ossa in 1969 to two immigrant parents from Colombia. When he started school, he did not know how to speak English. Due to his thirst for reading and education, he excelled in school. However, he was influenced by the mean streets of New York City and experienced all the obstacles and pitfalls that a young Latino experiences growing up in New York City. He went to law school passed the bar exam, and he is currently a trial attorney despite facing many of the obstacles that Latinos face in America.

The Secret Life of a First-Generation Latino Growing Up in New York City

Edwin Ossa

The Secret Life of a First-Generation Latino Growing Up in New York City

Olympia Publishers
London

www.olympiapublishers.com
OLYMPIA PAPERBACK EDITION

Copyright © Edwin Ossa 2024

The right of Edwin Ossa to be identified as author of
this work has been asserted in accordance with sections 77 and 78 of
the Copyright, Designs and Patents Act 1988.

All Rights Reserved

No reproduction, copy or transmission of this publication
may be made without written permission.
No paragraph of this publication may be reproduced,
copied or transmitted save with the written permission of the publisher,
or in accordance with the provisions
of the Copyright Act 1956 (as amended).

Any person who commits any unauthorized act in relation to
this publication may be liable to criminal
prosecution and civil claims for damage.

A CIP catalog record for this title is
available from the British Library.

ISBN: 978-1-80439-573-8

This book is a memoir. It reflects the author's present recollections of
experiences over time. Some names and characteristics have been
changed, some events have been compressed, and some dialogue
has been recreated.

First Published in 2024

Olympia Publishers
Tallis House
2 Tallis Street
London
EC4Y 0AB

Printed in Great Britain

Dedication

I dedicate this book to my wife, Sandy, and our two sweet.
Beautiful girls, Christina and Liliana Ossa.

Acknowledgments

Thank you, Mommy, for giving me the inspiration and strength from heaven to write this book.

CHAPTER 1

Growing up as a First-Generation Latino in New York City was exciting, fun, scary, depressing, exhilarating and frustrating, but never boring. Exactly what does First-Generation mean? To me, it means that I was the first person born in the United States from a family that can trace their lineage back to the ancient civilizations of the Aztecs, Incas and Mayans. When you think about those great civilizations and what they accomplished it makes me feel proud. Unfortunately, America today does not have the same point of view.

As a Colombian American and a trial attorney in New York City, I always reflect back to my childhood when I am preparing for jury selection and trial. Serving as a defense attorney for a national insurance company that represents Fortune five hundred companies, if I let myself get intimidated or bullied in court I can get hit for millions. It is imperative that an attorney before any trial – criminal or civil – select the right jurors. I often have to speak to people from all walks of life during jury selection, including immigrants and First-Generation Latinos like me. I am proud that I can understand their perspective and be able to relate to them in a way that makes them feel comfortable and accepted. I will never forget where I came from or who I am, despite any success I may have as an attorney.

Growing up as a First-Generation Latino in New York City meant being beaten up by notorious gang members, having my life threatened on multiple occasions, being mugged and violated, getting beaten to within an inch of my life by New York City police officers, having to wear hand-me-down clothing, growing up in roach- and rat-infested apartments, being forced to grow up faster than I wanted to, surviving a potential drug overdose and being mocked because of my ethnicity.

It all began when my mother, María del Carmen Campo Bejarano Vélez, came to the United States in the late 1960s to work in Houston, Texas, as a nanny for a wealthy family that sponsored her trip to the United States from Cali, Colombia. She had been on a waiting list for two years as part of a work abroad program in Colombia. She was finally accepted after waiting for what felt like forever, and she was only twenty-two years old when she decided to take the risk and leave her family behind. She had studied business administration and bookkeeping in Colombia. She had a happy family life and a good upbringing, but she was adventurous and wanted the opportunities that the United States could offer. She had stars in her eyes and often dreamed about coming to America. Colombia was a developing country with limited upward mobility and opportunities for women in general and especially for educated women. Despite speaking limited English and with little money in her pocketbook, she made the pilgrimage to Houston, Texas.

My mother was very pretty and I am sure that when she arrived, the wife and woman of the house, Betty Ann Jones – despite her initial altruism – did not want the young Colombian nanny to stay too long since she noticed that the man of the house, Real Estate magnate Johnny Lee Jones, was gazing at and talking a little too much to the pretty young Colombian girl. My mother was very fair-skinned and had light brown hair and green eyes. She looked European and no one would have thought that she was from Colombia. Some of the neighbors even wondered if the lovely young nanny was related to the Jones family in some way. It is now more common knowledge that South American and Latino women are beautiful and come in all sizes, shapes and colors. The present-day Western world is familiar with Raquel Welch (real name Jo Raquel Tejada), Rita Hayworth (Margarita Carmen Cansino), Alexis Bledel, Linda Carter (Linda Jean Cordova), Sophia Vergara, Jennifer Lopez, Demi Lovato, Jessica Alba, Shakira (Shakira Isabel Mebarak Ripoll) and many others. It is unbelievable that back in the '60s, Hollywood would not even cast a Latina actress to play the role of Maria in the classic movie *West Side Story*, one of the greatest plays ever adapted into a movie. Natalie Wood was chosen to play Maria, even though she was not Latina.

After my mother was politely asked to leave by Mrs. Jones, she was given severance pay and she decided to move to New York City. She had cousins that she could stay with temporarily and she knew that she could make a new life for herself now that she was armed with a visa and could become a United States citizen. My mom moved to New York and brought her mother (my Abuelita Aura) and her grandmother (my Bisabuela Hortencia) with her from Colombia. Shortly after she arrived, she met my father, Jesús Antonio Ossa, through mutual friends, one of whom was my father's cousin, Jairo. They met during an ice-skating party in New York City's Central Park in the winter of 1969.

My father came to the United States with twenty dollars in his pocket and a temporary travel visa. He was only twenty-two years old and had taught himself how to speak English by watching American movies in the local theater in the small town of Sevilla, Colombia, where he grew up. He had lived on his own from age fourteen and had worked as an apprentice to a shoemaker to support himself in Colombia. My father dropped out of school in the fifth grade because he was lefthanded and his teachers would try to force him to write with his right hand. He often was ridiculed by his classmates and hit by his teachers with rulers or leather straps for failing to learn how to write with his right hand and for being defiant. In medieval Europe, lefthanders were considered evil, which was a belief accepted by the Catholic Church. During the Spanish Inquisition, left-handers were punished, tortured, and accused of consorting with the devil and of being witches or warlocks. It is hard to believe that centuries later, being lefthanded was still considered taboo in the small town of Sevilla, Colombia.

When my father came home from school, things did not get much better for him. My grandfather, Abuelito Hector, verbally and physically abused my father throughout most of his childhood. My father was constantly hit with a horsewhip or forced to crawl on his bare knees over raw rice on the concrete kitchen floor. The corporal punishment wouldn't stop until my father's blood stained the floor or he fell to the ground when his knees could no longer take the abrasions.

My father could not take the mental and physical abuse any longer, so he left the house at fourteen years old and moved to Bogotá, the capital city of Colombia, where he had to scratch and claw to support himself. When he woke up in the morning, he always wanted to be anywhere but home. Suicide was not an option back then, but I am sure the thought had crossed his mind. He rented a room with other young men and lived independently until he left Colombia. When he was finally able to obtain a temporary travel visa, he came to the United States looking for a different and less stressful life. My poor father was never able to act like a teenager or have any fun because he was too busy hustling and working to try to support himself. When he arrived, he was able to stay with his cousin Jairo, who lived in New York City. The travel visa was only good for one month and my father had every intention to go back to Colombia.

My mother and father had two distinct paths that led them to the United States, but fate brought them together. They met, dated and quickly conceived a child in what can only be described as love at first sight, followed by a whirlwind romance. They were married in May of 1969, and I was born on November 17, 1969. There was no question that my mother would have the baby and my father did not think twice about getting married. There would be no going back to Colombia for my father. My First-Generation Latino story began on November 16, 1969, when María del Carmen Campo Bejarano Vélez began having contractions. You may ask yourself, why so many last names? Perhaps some sage Latino or wise elder has a profound answer; however, all I know is that it is a Latino custom to hold onto last names from both sides of the family. For the baby boomers, we were called Hispanic, for the millennials it is Latino. As long as it is not *spic*! This is the ultimate derogatory word used for Latinos, but it is not widely used or acknowledged. In fact, I have not heard that insidious word in decades. Times are changing for the better; we are still divided racially, but not as overtly as in the past. Discriminatory hiring practices and favoritism based on race in the workforce are stronger than ever. Even though some minorities are outraged about racial epithets, Latinos just keep moving along. For the most part, Latinos don't complain or jump up and down every time someone says something derogatory, or if something derogatory about our culture is spewed on TV or in the media. I am proud of that aspect of our culture.

Generally, Latinos don't complain because they are too busy

working and taking care of their families. The immigrant Latinos are working hard, picking fruits and vegetables for Americans to enjoy at their local grocery stores, or mowing their lawns. They don't have a platform to complain but they struggle and fight to make a better life for their kids. Many immigrants are illegal, but why is that? Wasn't the United States the country that took in all the poor, hungry and impoverished immigrants? When the immigrants' skin color started getting darker and the language and culture became different, the doors suddenly closed. Even in all your favorite restaurants, most of the kitchen staff and cooks are Latino, but not the chef. Illegal Latinos are allegedly "stealing jobs" from Americans but if all the illegal Latinos were deported it would have a disastrous effect on the United States economy. Many Latinos – including Latinos that are undocumented – perform essential functions and hold down jobs that nobody else wants to perform. They utilize very few of the available government services: one stereotype that tends to be true is that Latinos have large extended families, which serve as safety nets and support systems.

    On the morning of November 16, 1969, my mother began having contractions in the Ossa family's one-bedroom apartment in Jackson Heights, Queens, New York. That morning my aunt, Diana, grandmother Aura, great-grandmother Hortencia, father Jesús Antonio and little cousin David left the apartment to go to the hospital. Yes, we all lived in the same apartment. I am not sure what the sleeping arrangements were back then, but I would say it would be taking the phrase "close-knit family" to another level. Elmhurst Hospital, which was within walking distance from our one-bedroom palace, did not accept immigrants without health insurance unless it was deemed an emergency. Surprisingly, my birth was not deemed as an emergency. It seems that you had to have been shot or literally dying to be admitted without health insurance. Many decades later, my best friend's little brother Benny was examined at Elmhurst Hospital, the same hospital that turned my family down back in 1969. He was just feeling faint and did not think it was necessary to go to a more renowned hospital. After an alleged thorough examination in the emergency room, the medical personnel cleared Benny and declared that he was fit to go home. He was in his early twenties with no significant past medical history. In fact, his mother and brother were well off, and money and health insurance were not an issue. Benny had a darker complexion than most Latinos and despite being well educated, smarter than most regardless of ethnicity, and financially secure, he was labeled and lumped in with all the rest of the immigrant Latinos. The examination was cursory at best, and he was discharged with a clean bill of health. As he walked out of the hospital he collapsed and died. The family did not bring a lawsuit against the hospital because they were Christian and did not want to be involved in prolonged litigation that would bring back constant bad memories. They chose to forgive and forget and turn the other cheek. They concluded that it was God's will. However, it was a tragedy that may not have happened in a hospital in a more upscale neighborhood. The coroner's report, in what was an obvious attempt to protect the City Hospital and can only be described as a cover-up, concluded that Benny died of natural causes. I will never forget Benny: he was a smart, vibrant young man and I believe that he was destined for greatness. Poor Benny deserved better. This was an unbelievable tragedy.

Returning to my mother and my birth: the entire family was present when she began having contractions. So, the entire clan packed a few things and headed to St. Luke's Roosevelt Hospital, which was located in what is called the Hell's Kitchen section of New York City. It was a safe neighborhood in the morning, but you did not want to be caught there at night because it would turn into hell. Recently, my wife saw what St. Luke's Roosevelt Hospital looked like in a movie that we watched together depicting St. Luke's near the time when I was born, in the early 1970s. She jokingly commented, "Damn, you were born in that shithole!" Back then how would a fetus respond to that? Maybe like this: "Yes, but there was nowhere to go but up!" St. Luke's Hospital accepted immigrants without health insurance with open arms.

You may wonder why everyone in the family went to the hospital, once again it is a Latino custom. Not only did my immediate family go to the hospital but among the others that went were my father's cousin Jairo and his wife Damaris, cousin Alonso and his wife Sandy, cousin Livardo and one of his many girlfriends, family friend Roman, cousin Jaime and his lover Alfredo. Livardo's nickname was el Mejicano (the Mexican) because he was dark-skinned, used to like wearing cowboy hats and cowboy boots and used to tell everyone that he was Mexican. That's all that I can recall from my mother's stories, but I am sure that there were even more relatives and family friends that showed up. Ironically, in 1969, many of my relatives and family that I am closest with today were still in the mother country, Colombia.

My family did not have a car or money for a cab. Back then no one even thought about calling an ambulance, so the journey began in the New York City subway system. The family all rushed to the 90th street train station of the elevated number 7 train. From the number 7 train, they all transferred at the 74th

Street station to the E train, then to the 1 train at Times Square to the 59th Street station. As the Ossa clan emerged from the subway into the street in 1969 Hell's Kitchen on the way to the hospital, even the hustlers, pimps, drug dealers, and street walkers gazed in amazement at the young Latino woman who looked like she was ready to pop. They all stepped aside and the Hell's Kitchen sidewalk leading to the hospital was reminiscent of the scene in the iconic movie *The Ten Commandments* or the passage in the Bible where Moses parts the Red Sea. Having been born and raised in New York City, today I know the New York City trains like the back of my hand. Obviously at that time I was not even born yet, but I give my parents credit because finding your way around New York City can get complicated.

My birth was as complicated as the New York City subway system. My parents told me that I was born prematurely and that I almost died. I was born with an abnormally big head, and I was born blue, yes literally, shockingly blue! Baby boy blue with bumps all over my head. For those of you that remember the old 1980s cartoon, I looked like a damn Smurf. I was placed in an incubator, where I lived for weeks. I had serious respiratory issues because I developed bronchitis and then pneumonia. It was touch and go for some time. Later in life, I realized that I was not premature since my parents' wedding anniversary was in May and I was born in November. Obviously, I was not born three months premature. I probably would have died if I had been premature since my birth was difficult even though I was born on time. I finally figured it out when I was older, and my parents just gave me a wry smile when I confronted them with the math. Back in their day, premarital sex was taboo, so it was better to tell your son that he was born prematurely than to tell him the truth. Things became even more complicated because my neurotic parents were concerned about my oversized head, so they had me tested by a pediatric neuropsychologist. The cognitive tests revealed that my brain was working just fine; I just happened to be a small baby with an abnormally big head.

After I was born, we moved from our one-bedroom palace a few blocks from Denman Street in Elmhurst Queens, to 88th Street and Roosevelt Avenue in Jackson Heights, Queens. Geographically, it was a move from one side of the 7 train elevated tracks to the other side, but it was not an upgrade because both sides of the tracks were equally bad. Usually there is one good side when you talk about the other side of the tracks. In our neighborhood, one side had drugs, prostitution and violence, the other side had gangs, shady stores and illegal businesses that were drug fronts and money laundering operations. I was just a child, but I always wondered why there would be a real estate agency right on Roosevelt Avenue underneath the elevated 7 train, between 88th Street and 89th Street. Who would be crazy enough to go there to see a real estate agent to help them find a house or an apartment? Buying a house or finding a place to live is one of the most important things that any family can do and one of the biggest financial commitments that any family will ever undertake. Who would go to a real estate agency located on the block where people were often robbed, raped, mugged, and killed on a regular basis? When I was growing up, I never saw any police officers on that block or in my entire neighborhood. Perhaps they were bribed to look the other way or just didn't care about us. When you are raised in such a neighborhood, all the violence and mayhem seem normal. A lot of this mayhem had ties to Pablo Escobar one of the mosr notorious drug lords in the history of the world.

One summer day when I was about eight years old, a group

of men were shooting dice on the sidewalk on Roosevelt Avenue, at the corner of the block where I lived. I was going to my best friend Mario's house on 89th Street, a block away from my building. As I walked toward these nefarious men, I could see pistol handles sticking out from some of these men's pants, by their waistlines. Even at that young age, I was always noticing things. I knew it was a rough-and-tumble neighborhood even at eight years old, but I didn't think anything of it. I was always good at board games that involved having to roll dice, especially Parcheesi. I hated to lose at anything and even then, I was always super competitive. I secretly wondered if they would let me play. These men were playing craps.

As I walked to my friend's house, I stopped to look at what was going on and became mesmerized. I wanted to play so badly, and it was almost as if I willed it to happen. As I was staring at them play, suddenly one of the men yelled: "Hey kid, why don't you take my spot? I'm having bad luck today." The other men started cursing and yelling in Spanish and English. I heard curse words in both languages that I never had heard before. I wasn't scared but I was extremely excited, and my heart was racing. My new scary friend touched the handle of his pistol, and everyone shut the hell up. He wrapped his arm around me and told me, "Don't worry kid, I have a feeling." I had never played craps before, but he explained what I needed to roll in order to win. I went on a hot streak and I was rolling the dice for what seemed like hours. I felt a rush of adrenaline that I had never felt before in my young life. My new friend was making a great deal of money. I kept watching him pick up a lot of bills after my rolls. I had only seen small bills in my young life but that afternoon I saw big bills that I had never seen before. I started to get nervous because I had to be home soon; if I broke curfew my dad would hit me with the belt. That was the usual form of punishment for many immigrant kids in the inner city. I told my new friend that I had to leave, and he was upset. I think he understood though because he said, "Here you go," and stuffed a bunch of bills into my hand. The wad was so big I could barely hold onto it. At that young age I didn't realize how much money I was handed but it was in the thousands. He laughed hysterically and told me, "Buy some candy or whatever the hell you kids like these days, but don't tell your mother!"

I was so thrilled that I ran home and told my mother I was going to buy something nice for her. She said: "Hijo (son), I know you will one day."

I was so excited that I said, "No, Mami, not one day, today!" I showed her all the money and she almost fainted.

She exclaimed, "Where did you get all that money?"

I replied, "Mami, I won it fair and square."

She demanded, "Take me to where you won it before your father gets home. He is going to hit you and punish you if he finds out."

We went to the corner and the men were still playing. I could see the look of disgust on my new friend's face as we approached. Despite my pleas, my mother made me give all the money back. My new friend cursed at me in Spanish and called me a pendejo (idiot). He growled, "I told you not to tell your mother!" My mom was mad and argued with these men, and they yelled at both of us and cursed us out. I thought I would have deserved a bit more respect since I won so much money for that man. So I learned at a young age that there was no respect in the streets of Jackson Heights.

As a young Latino, I lived with my mother, father and abuelitas. However, my abuelitas basically ran the house and raised me while my parents were working. My Bisabuela Hortencia was my rock. She loved me unconditionally and to this day I still miss her. Growing up as a young Latino boy in the 1970s, I felt a lot of racism but because of the way I grew up it did not matter since I was taught to just work hard and keep it moving. I was bullied and made fun of because I spoke limited English as a young boy. When I started school at PS89, I did not speak English. I know that mainstream Americans are often judgmental about immigrant parents not speaking English to their kids, but I actually appreciated it. My abuelitas and my parents spoke to me in Spanish, so I learned how to speak Spanish well.

I learned how to read and speak English in school and by watching PBS and educational shows like *Sesame Street*, *The Electric Company* and *Mr. Rogers' Neighborhood* on television. These shows were not only entertaining, but also helped develop my language skills. With their help, by the 3rd grade I went from English as a Second Language classes to honors classes. To this day, I take proper grammar and enunciation as a source of pride.

Growing up in the hood has different meanings for different people. There is a celebrity actor/comedian, John Leguizamo, who grew up in Jackson Heights a few blocks from where I used to live, at about the same time that I lived there. In his comedy sets, he talks about how hardcore his neighborhood was. It makes me laugh because I grew up in the same neighborhood and for me it just brings back good memories. Perhaps he was at a boarding school while I was enjoying my youth in the hood. Just to be clear, some things were a little rough and kids shouldn't have to deal with such things, but that's just what we knew and how we grew up in the streets. When I was about eight years old, my buddy Mario's gang friend wanted to send a message to a rival gang member. He beat up this kid and then we dragged him into a building basement. We tied him up to a chair in the basement of the building across from where Mario lived. It seemed like all those buildings had desolate, long, dark, cavernous basements. I always wondered if anyone had the courage to go down to those basements that had decrepit laundry rooms. I believe most people in the neighborhood went to public laundromats, which were always packed. Over the years many murder and criminal investigations would lead to those neighborhood basements. After we tied him to the chair, Mario's friend – the gang member – grabbed a towel and rubbed dog shit on it and wrapped it around this poor kid's face and tied it up across his face. He then took out a knife from his waistband and told us to get the fuck out of there. The basement area where we tied him up was abandoned and littered with all types of garbage and waste including dog feces. We left him tied up to that chair. My heart was racing, and I was too young to truly understand what was going on, but I still cannot believe some of the things we did back then in the old neighborhood. I didn't tell my parents because I knew that my father would beat me within an inch of my life. The gang member warned me that if I told anyone what he did that he would kill me. That was the first time that anyone had threatened my life. He didn't have to threaten me because I felt a misguided loyalty to my neighborhood friends. I would turn nine years old in about four months.

There were also those times when my neighborhood friends used to terrorize commuters on the subway. These unhinged kids I used to hang out with had no conscience or remorse and would terrorize innocent people. One time they harassed a passenger on the 7 train because he had a foreign accent. He was a grown man and they mocked him; he was carrying an umbrella and they beat him with his own umbrella. I thought to myself, wow that could be someone's father. When this poor man came home from work, how could he look his family in the face and explain why he had so many bruises? People don't understand what happens when there is a mob frenzy. Why didn't he just fight back or defend himself against a bunch of kids? I was there but I did not actively participate. However, if this guy fought back, I would have been expected to get involved because that was the code. I know this sounds terrible but that's just how I grew up in the streets of Jackson Heights and even back then I knew that it was wrong.

CHAPTER 2

Growing up in the hood could be fun and exciting. However, now that I have kids, I would not want them growing up the way I did. Maybe that sounds hypocritical, but I think a lot of people who grew up in the hood would want their children to have a better childhood than they did. I must say, though, that living on 88th Street next to the elevated train track was always interesting. When I was very young, we lived in a building on Roosevelt Avenue on the fifth floor, very close to the 7 elevated train track and every time the train passed by, the entire apartment would shake. The subway tracks were so close that it seemed that if I opened the kitchen window in the apartment I could reach out and touch those tracks. The only thing I can compare it to was living next to a roller coaster. To say that it was loud and intense would be an understatement. Navigating through breakfast at the kitchen table was always an adventure.

There were also a lot of cockroaches and rats in that building. Even though my abuelitas kept our apartment spotless, sadly the rats and cockroaches would come in through the windows, burrow through the walls and even squeeze under the doors. No amount of cleaning could ever stop them. They were as inescapable as zombies in horror movies that show the living dead invading in droves. Think about a scary episode of the AMC cable series "The Walking Dead"! Of all the vivid memories that I have about the hood, these memories of infestations are the ones I would prefer to forget. I was eating cereal one morning and I noticed little brown spots in the bowl. It was Frosted Flakes, not Raisin Bran! I found out later that the little brown spots were baby cockroaches. One of the worst scenes of my childhood occurred when I walked into our apartment with my father one afternoon and we saw a rat sitting defiantly in the walkway leading to the living room. I freaked out but my hardcore father did not even flinch. He grew up in Sevilla, Colombia, during the "Era de Violencia" (Violence Era), a ten-year civil war and he became accustomed to seeing blood and dead bodies in the local river. My father stomped on that rat with his dress shoes. I saw the guts squirt out from the sides of the rat and I heard a high-pitched shriek that to this day I can't seem to get out of my head. He calmly took a paper towel and scraped the rat and guts off the floor and threw it into the garbage pail in the kitchen. I loved that about my father: he was fearless. I wish I could have seen the look on my mother's and abuelita's faces when they opened the trash basket and saw that disgusting blend of smashed rat, blood and guts. Ooooh, ¿eso qué es? What is that? Yuck!

Fast forward thirty-five years. A lot has changed: my abuelitas and my mother have passed away, and the Ossa family has drifted apart. My dad and my aunts moved to Florida. My mother was the glue that kept the family together, so once she passed away, all the old relatives and family friends went their own separate ways. My sister Valeria planned a family trip to try to rekindle the Ossa family flames and bring us back together. I love my sister, but of course the trip was a disaster. She rented a house in Lancaster, Pennsylvania, a place known for the Amish, an old-school religious group that follows a traditional way of living. When visitors go to Lancaster to see the Amish and their traditional lifestyle as tourists you are supposed to enjoy the horse and buggies, the outfits, the crafts and everything associated with classic culture and American treasure. You're not supposed to try to live like the old-fashioned Amish! My sister rented a house that was approximately two hundred and fifty years old, and it looked like it had never been renovated or refurbished. The irony is that there was a nice Hilton Hotel less than a block away.

The house was dusty, dingy and scary looking. I have always been in tune with the supernatural, which is a characteristic that has existed on both sides of my family for centuries. I knew that there were spirits in the house – I could feel them. The house was definitely haunted! I wanted to leave immediately but I decided to try to make the best of it. The immediate family was staying there, including my father and his girlfriend, my sister Valeria and her husband and daughter, my lovely niece Tati, my Tía Carmen and her mom Margarita, my wife Sandy and my two beautiful girls Christina and Liliana – we were all crowded into that rickety old, haunted house.

On that first night, we all gathered in the kitchen and began playing dominos, the game of choice for old-school Latinos. Despite the less-than-desirable accommodation, we chose a distraction and tried to have some fun. It was summertime and the heat was sweltering, so we kept the kitchen door open. We were living like the Amish – whether we liked it or not – since of course there was no air conditioning. As we were playing dominos, I noticed a shadowy dark figure fly in through the kitchen door and swoop toward me. At first I thought it was a spirit or a demon. Then I felt a furry creature bang into my leg. It happened too fast for me to react. Of course, I freaked out and became hysterical. It brought back bad memories of the rat at Jackson Heights. After the creature bounced off my leg, we all realized that it was a bat. The whole family was screaming and freaking out as that bat was flying all over the place. My intrepid father, then in his seventies and suffering from arthritis, immediately grabbed a broom, chased the bat and swatted him down. He then grasped the broom handle and skewered the wretched bat. I heard a loud piercing shriek. He then calmly grabbed a paper towel, scooped up the bat and the bat guts and threw it into the trash basket in the kitchen. It certainly made me feel like a kid again! Yuck!

Living in the hood was always entertaining. In the summer back in the '70s all you had to do for fun was look out the window, and you would see knife and gun fights between the CC boys and Rockers Revenge, the two local rival gangs. I remember seeing the neighborhood drunk "Auita" stumbling around all the time. Why was he called Auita? It comes from "agua," which means water in Spanish, plus "ita," the diminutive suffix. Whoever came up with this nickname either erased or swallowed the g, and called him Auita, because he was always drinking alcohol as if it were water. People in the neighborhood would egg him on and yell out "Auita, Auita" and he would smile and pick up his pace. His cheeks were always rosy red, and he had fair skin and sandy blond hair, but he was Latino, not Irish. From a white American perspective, he looked like Howdy Doody, an old classic children's show character. The only difference was that Auita spoke Spanish and he was always drunk. In all the years of my youth growing up in Jackson Heights, I never saw him sober, but he always looked happy. Perhaps he was living on a disability pension or a lawsuit settlement. Auita was always stumbling around with an open container or just singing in the streets. Nobody looked down on him as he was always smiling and laughing. Auita was always entertaining; he was the ghetto clown. I wish I knew his back story or what became of him. There was no YouTube or internet back then, but gazing out of my window was all the entertainment I needed.

As a youth, I always romanticized about joining the CC Boys. I stupidly believed that joining a gang would give me street cred and a sense of belonging. The CC Boys were "the baddest motherfuckers" in the neighborhood. When one of my best childhood friends, Charlie, told me that his teenage sister had been viciously raped by Ozzy, a leader of the CC Boys who lived in the building, that traumatized me and turned me away from the CC Boys and everything that gang life represented. I realized the vicious nature and harsh reality of being a member of a street gang. When the police stormed into our building like an army invading enemy territory during a war, I saw Ozzy being taken away in handcuffs by what looked like an endless number of armed police officers. "Damn!" I thought, "there goes the guy who raped my good friend's older sister!" I had an innocent crush on her. It was very hard for kids to maintain any kind of innocence in the hood.

When I was ten years old, I got into a fight with Lario, one of the leaders of the CC Boys. Lario was in his late teens, and he was a "badass dude" who was feared and well-known in the neighborhood as someone you shouldn't mess with. He disrespected me on the street one afternoon when I was with my cousin David. He slapped me on the back of the head for no reason. I can't remember why he did that, other than just to bully me, but he disrespected me and was making fun of me. David was actually egging him on – yes, my own cousin! – to try to gain favor with Lario. I don't know where I mustered the courage, but I knew what I had to do. I didn't threaten Lario or talk back to him, I just made the decision to walk up to him slowly and surprise him by punching him in the stomach as hard as I could.

He doubled over, as he wasn't expecting me to do that. Then as he doubled over, I kicked him in the face and threw him down to the floor. I wanted to continue hitting him, but I knew that if I didn't kill him, he would come after me with his gang soldiers. I did not finish the job, but my cowardly cousin helped him up and apologized. I no longer had the element of surprise on my side. Once he caught his breath, he raced toward me and continuously punched and slapped me as hard as he could. I felt a stinging sensation in my mouth and all over my face. I could taste blood in my mouth and my face felt like it was on fire. I was on the verge of losing consciousness and rather than jump in to help me, David, who was four years older than me, continued to apologize to Lario and took me away quickly. I tried to rush Lario again, but David held me back. Lario just laughed – a long, loud laugh. As he left, he said, "Hey, at least the little man has heart." Lario would be convicted of murder a few years later and perhaps my cousin David saved my life.

David took me to his mom's (my Tía Diana's) apartment and put cold water on my face, trying to wipe off some of the blood and make my bruised and bloody face look better. My parents and my aunt found out about the beating, and they were very upset. David said that it was my fault and I brought it upon myself. As punishment, my dad hit me with the belt. I got beaten up by Lario within an inch of my life and then, as a reward, I got beaten again by my father. It was a vicious cycle, like when my dad was beaten at school and then at home. The funny thing is that I was always fearless and not scared to fight, but I wanted more out of life than just being a thug. I honestly have to thank my parents for that.

  I used to hang out with a lot of tough kids in the old neighborhood, but I never felt that I ever truly belonged or fit in.

After all these years and an education including a psychology degree, I realize that perhaps some of my friends may have been sociopaths. If these were my friends, what does that say about me? I think that I was always in survival mode growing up in the hood. I advertently or inadvertently aligned myself with the toughest kids in the neighborhood. Growing up nobody ever messed with me in grade school or junior high school. I was always friends with the toughest and scariest kids. I used to hide from my friends the fact that I loved to read. I used to sneak to the local library in the morning and then hang out with my gang friends in the afternoon. They never knew that before I was ten years old, I had read all the classics: *Tom Sawyer*, *Moby Dick*, *A Connecticut Yankee in King Arthur's Court*, *The Raven*, *Romeo and Juliet* and many others. Shakespeare was challenging but I was able to figure out the context and the meanings behind the scenes. At a young age, I realized how powerful literature could be.

I went to PS89 (PS stands for public school), which was a typical inner-city New York elementary school. Just like most inner-city schools in New York City back then, and even to this day, it was overcrowded and underfunded. The school playground was basically the streets surrounding the school building since there was no designated playground. The school building took up all the space, except for a small trailer next to the school that looked like an RV, where kindergarten classes were held. There would be police barriers closing the street where the school was located during school hours, but I never saw any police officers anywhere near the school. Across the street from the school were residential rent control buildings, basically low-income housing, and you could imagine the types of people that lived in those buildings. On the one hand, there were solid immigrant families trying to raise their kids and extended families. However, there were also unsavory and shady criminal types that lived there because it was affordable and cheap. Those buildings and our school were on the same block. We played games like tag, freeze tag and manhunt during recess. There were parked cars in the street, and we would jump on top of them to try to avoid being caught while we played during our lunch break.

One of my fondest memories is jumping on top of the hood of a car and diving into a pile of my teammates and freeing them from manhunt jail during a game of manhunt. Whoever parked on that block must have been either uninformed or crazy because I am sure a lot of dents were caused by rowdy kids during recess. We were running around during recess and unsavory characters – possibly even pedophiles and murderers – would be leaving their buildings and walking past the school saying inappropriate things to us. Once during my lunch break, I was told to "get the fuck outta here" by some scary-looking dude exiting one of the buildings. Tenants would curse and yell at us from their windows. Children should not be exposed to that. If anyone tried to find the teacher aides to complain, the aides would either be missing in action, (probably going to their homes or nearby restaurants for lunch) or taking smoking breaks in areas where the kids could not see them. I don't remember much adult supervision during recess. All types of mayhem would go on during recess, including kids kissing, fighting, bullying, stealing lunch money, extortion and overall bedlam. Then after about half an hour some authority figure would show up and blow a whistle very loudly. I was involved in many fights at school and came home bloodied with no questions asked because my abuelita Hortencia would always clean me up before my father came home. It makes me laugh that all these fights took place, and the school personnel were missing in action. It was an unwritten code that win or lose we were not going to snitch. Teacher aides would appear mysteriously, and we would be told to calm down and get in line so that we could all go back to school in an orderly fashion.

Talk about survival of the fittest – this was Darwinism in the hood! The age range at the school was five to ten years old. You had to make alliances, protect yourself, not let yourself get "punk'd," not let other kids disrespect you, tolerate lunch food that was barely edible and not fit for humans let alone growing kids, survive nut allergies because no one ever heard of that back then and basically just try to make it through the day in one piece. Early on in life, I found out the hard way that I was allergic to nuts. I had a severe nut allergy attack that included my throat closing and intense vomiting. My parents had to rush me to the hospital. Thank God I was at home because if I was at school during my lunch break with those absentee lunch aides, I would have died. Once the lunch meal consisted of cheeseburgers that had a green tint to them, and it was not a special holiday meal for St. Patrick's Day. We were all children of poor immigrants, so we were stuck with the cafeteria lunch because it was free. The irony is that when we went home, we would eat great food, probably better than today's kids because regardless of ethnicity, the food and the cooking at home was always good. First-Generation kids were spoiled when it came to home cooking. Immigrant moms' and grandmas' cooking is appreciated in all cultures.

In elementary school, JoJo was one of my best friends. Thinking back, I don't even know what we had in common. He was just a real "bad ass." He lived in my building and his parents were Puerto Rican. One year he invited me to his birthday party at his apartment when he was turning nine years old. His father was serving a prison sentence for armed robbery and his older brothers were already criminals. His mother wanted better for JoJo. I believe that party was a microcosm of JoJo's life. At the party, one of Jojo's older brothers put on music that JoJo didn't like. JoJo defiantly yelled, "it's my party – take that fucking shit off," and his older brother pushed him and JoJo fell on the record player. The record player went flying and JoJo ended up on his back on the floor. JoJo immediately sprang up and threw himself on his older brother, who was a teenager and much bigger than him and punched his older brother in the lip, causing him to bleed. I jumped in to prevent the brother from beating him up, and then his mother told us all to "get the fuck out of her house." I was just following the code; without thinking about the ramifications, I had my boy's back no matter what. I am still dumbfounded by what happened that day. We were just kids, and we should have been at Chuck E Cheese or an amusement park, having fun. For JoJo's birthday there was no cake, no opening presents and no blowing out candles.

After we were thrown out of the apartment, we went to see our friend "Dracula," who had that nickname because he had two teeth that looked like fangs. The three of us were really tight. Dracula's real name was Robby and his mother was a prostitute/call girl. Robby was never ashamed or embarrassed and he always bragged about how much his mother loved him and bought him nice clothes. We used to go to Robby's house because his mom was never home. There was a hammock in his living room and a jar full of flavored and colored condoms. I was about eight years old when I learned what a condom was.

The summers were always fun. We couldn't go to camp or do anything that cost money, so we just invented our own fun.

There was an abandoned parking lot across the street from my building with a bunch of stray cats. JoJo, Dracula and I decided to grab one of those cats one hot lazy summer day and clean it up. We bathed the cat at Robby's place in the bathtub. His mom was not home as usual; she would have killed him if she knew that dirty cat was in her bathtub. All types of fleas and who knows what else came off that alley cat's fur. After we cleaned the alley cat, we went to a local thrift store and stole a bunch of ribbons and decorated the stray cat. Then we went all over the neighborhood trying to sell it. Nobody wanted to buy it and we were cursed out and told to leave those stray alley cats alone. JoJo threatened to beat up a few people before we finally gave up on our great cat enterprise.

One afternoon we went to visit one of Dracula's friends that JoJo and I didn't know, a boy named Ryan. We showed up at his apartment and his parents weren't home. Now I think it's sad – although I didn't think so back then – that many of these kids had parents who were never home and who let their kids run around unsupervised. Ryan came out in a bathrobe and was acting strangely, so I already knew that trouble was brewing. Ryan had a German Shepherd. He went into the kitchen and took out a jar of peanut butter. He then proceeded to spread the peanut butter all over his private parts. His dog then licked all the peanut butter from his privates. I didn't know how to react or what to think. I just knew what was coming: JoJo beat the hell out of Ryan. JoJo was such a "bad ass" that the dog got scared and ran away and hid under Ryan's bed, whimpering. Ryan was lying on the ground, crying, with his bathrobe open and peanut butter all over the place, and that's the last time I ever saw Ryan. I ran out of there I don't know what elso JoJo did to him but he told me to never talk about the fact that we went to Ryan's house that day

On the Fourth of July 1980, we bought illegal fireworks, just as all the inner-city kids did and continue to do. Somebody from the neighborhood always had a connection, either from down south or in Chinatown. We were always able to buy firecrackers, M80s and pineapples, which were like mini dynamite sticks. We used to hang out a lot on the roof of my friend Mario's building on 89th Street. It was like another turf, as we were all territorial back then. JoJo and Dracula lived on my block, and we generally did not hang out with anyone from outside the block, but Mario had been my friend since I was very young, and I considered him my brother from another mother. We were playing with the M80s, which had short fuses. We would light the fuses with matches and then lob them off the roof down to the street. It didn't occur to us knuckleheads that we could have blown our hands or fingers off! Youth is certainly wasted on the young. I hope that no passerby was ever hurt below. I never felt comfortable doing that, but I did succumb to the inner-city peer pressure.

 I recall that Fourth of July, JoJo stuffed a pack of firecrackers into some kid's back pocket. He told that kid that if he took it out, he was going to "kick his ass." By that summer, JoJo had developed a notorious reputation in the neighborhood. The kid was so scared – even though he was bigger, older and taller than JoJo – that he kept it in his back pocket. JoJo then lit a fuse on one of the firecrackers in the pack and the whole thing went off in this poor kid's back pocket. He was jumping up and down, screaming and crying hysterically. His rear end was on fire while those firecrackers went off one by one! I never saw that kid again around the neighborhood. This was the last summer before JoJo was locked up. He was adjudicated as a juvenile delinquent and spent time in a juvenile detention facility. I never found out exactly what JoJo was locked up for, but I am sure it was really bad because I never saw him again after that summer. I found out years later that he had graduated from juvenile delinquency and was convicted as an adult for armed robbery and felony assault.

 Mario was my best childhood friend. He had a younger sister, Hannah, who always liked me; I never thought about her in a romantic kind of way, but I liked her too. Secretly, one of my fond memories is of Mario's mom scantily clad whenever I went to visit him. She didn't do anything on purpose, she just liked to be comfortable in her apartment. We were all so young that I am sure she didn't think anything of it. Just like any pre-teen back then, I was a horny kid. When I was about six or seven years old, I noticed that if you placed your penis under the bathtub faucet, the stream of water would give you a funny but euphoric sensation. I was having orgasms without knowing what they were. I remember my abuelita came in on me in the bathroom once and I hid my penis with a toy dinosaur. She yelled at me and told me I was going to go blind. I guess different cultures have different variations of these urban legends. Let's just say I was always clean and smelled fresh as a young boy. Unfortunately, in the hood, we grew up too fast. I was playing spin the bottle and making out with girls before I was even ten years old. I guess all of us had working parents and were left to our own devices. Hannah's friend Claudia invited us to her house for a "play date." It was not like today's play dates, but more like a make-out and show-and-tell session. We were just kids, with no adults present and we did what puberty pushed us to do. I was so young that I did not even have the ability to ejaculate. We took off our clothes, jumped in the bed and kissed and fondled each other. We were too young to understand the potential consequences of our adolescent love making. Now that I have two young daughters, I cringe about what we were doing.

CHAPTER 3

Back in the late 70s, sports and games in the hood were different from what anybody could ever imagine today. In the summer it seemed that the humidity was supercharged, especially in the concrete jungle. Someone's older brother or father would open a fire hydrant and someone else would cover it with a cap or cloth with holes, to create a sprinkling effect. The kids on the block would run around on the street, getting sprinkled until they were soaked. There were no permits or anything resembling legal access. I am sure if the proper steps were taken, the NYC Department of Environmental Protection (the city agency in charge of water, fire hydrants, water mains, etc.) would spend years evaluating whether to allow the hydrants to be opened for public use. Fortunately for us, protocols and rules were not followed in the hood, so we had a lot of fun running around in the spraying water, getting relief from the oppressive heat. There were no nearby swimming pools or beaches for the inner-city kids in my neighborhood. Most of us were being watched by our abuelitas or neighbors while our parents were working. It was a blessing that they could do other things or relax while we super-energized, overactive kids ran around in the water. Obviously, there was no dress code and I do remember some of these kids, especially the younger ones, running around either naked or in their underwear. Even babies with diapers were carried into the street to cool off under the sprinkling water. However, I should note that the play area by the fire hydrant was never truly sanitary. There could be leftover blood from the gang fights of the previous night, or shit from all the kids running around unsupervised for hours. I also remember seeing used condoms in the street, as well as scattered needles, evidence that the drug epidemic was beginning to explode in the late 70s.

As I got older the entertainment in the hood became more creative and dangerous, something like a mixture of the X Games and the Hunger Games. When I went to my friend Mario's block we would play a dangerous form of tag. There were two buildings in close proximity to each other, so we would jump from one roof to the other. The distance was several feet, and there was no net below, so if anyone tripped or fell in between the six-story buildings, the result would be a horrific injury or death. These are the kinds of stunts you see in iconic action movies like *Die Hard* and *Mission Impossible*, in which stuntmen perform the actual feats, not the actors.

Another game we played as kids was called the token game. We would hang out at the 90th Street 7 train station and rig the turnstiles. In those days tokens were used and not metro cards to get on the subway. There was a way to push the turnstile slightly forward and cause it to lock, and when someone put in their token the turnstile would remain locked. When a commuter approached, we would have to convince him that the turnstile was broken, and sneak him in. However, the token remained in the slot. Then we would have to convince the next commuter that our token was stuck and convince him to give us money. Afterward, he would pass through on the previous commuter's token. It wasn't easy because the commuters were very skeptical. Also, we could only do it for a limited amount of time because the MTA (Metropolitan Transit Authority) booth collector would see what we were doing and call the police. Whenever that happened, we would hop the turnstile and take the train to another station and keep up the scam until we made enough money or got bored and tired. The token game was played in the summer when we were on vacation, and we tried to do it early in the morning when people were going to work. They were in such a hurry that they didn't realize or care that they were being conned. On an average day we could make hundreds of dollars, which was a lot for us at the time. I don't think our Jackson Heights crew was the only one pulling that scam because all the NYC turnstiles were later remodeled. I am not proud of what we did – it was just part of growing up in the hood.

One summer day I was playing the token game at the last stop, Main Street – Flushing, a busy 7 train station. A transit cop saw what I was doing and ran toward me and told me to stop. As he approached me, I jumped the turnstile and ran down the subway steps. He must have radioed for backup because I saw a sea of blue chasing me all over the train station. I ran track for my junior high school team, and I was always very fast. I even broke the district record for the mile run. It didn't occur to me to turn myself in because my father would have beaten me to a pulp if I was arrested. I was more scared of my father than the police. I had all these cops chasing me and I could feel the heat of their breath on the back of my neck. No police officer was going to shoot a stupid Latino kid for scamming commuters, but they were determined to catch me, cuff me, and arrest me. I ran up the stairs and jumped back over the turnstile and up the exit stairs into the street. The police officers gave up the chase. The police were not going to call for squad cars or helicopters just to chase down a mischievous Latino kid. I kept running from that train station until I got home, a distance of about three miles. I had to run past Shea Stadium (now Citi Field), Flushing Meadow Park and the

USTA National Tennis Center, where the US Open is still played. It would have been a great sightseeing tour for a tourist. In the early 80s I never paid to take the subway. I still have nightmares about the MTA booth employees screaming into their microphones "Pay your fare." I felt guilty whenever I rode the trains with my parents because we would all pay our fares. They never discovered what I was doing when I was out with my neighborhood friends.

After playing the token game all morning during our summer vacations, we would take the 7 train to the last stop, Main Street – Flushing. Then we would take an MTA bus into Whitestone, New York. Whitestone was and continues to be an affluent community in Queens. There was a beautiful private pool that was open to the public but charged an expensive admission fee; my own parents couldn't even afford to take me there. The pool was more like a sports complex, with multiple pools and diving boards. Since we took the bus at the first stop on the bus route, there would always be a lot of people waiting in line. So, we would pry open the back door while everyone was paying to board the bus, and we would sneak in. As with the turnstiles, MTA buses were later remodeled. Perhaps our Jackson Heights crew can claim that we encouraged the MTA to make changes for the better. We would sometimes get caught, but usually the bus driver would only yell at us. If the driver stopped the bus or tried to come after us, we would jump out the back door. Most of the time we would get away with it. It felt kind of empowering to be able to travel all over New York City taking public transportation without paying. We had money from cashing in on the token game, but it was more fun to sneak in everywhere. Once we arrived at Whitestone we would head to the pool. To this day I am not sure what the exorbitant admission fee for the pool was.

One of the guys from our neighborhood crew knew a lifeguard that worked at the pool. He told us that there would never be any security in a certain back area of the complex. The only issue was that we had to scale a tall barbed-wire fence. That's when all the daredevil skills came in handy. We had to climb up near the top and then put one leg over the barbed wires and in one fell swoop pull over our other leg and jump down to the other side. If I tried to do that today I would impale myself and probably end up in the hospital.

Just like the X Games and the Winter Olympics, there were also winter games in the hood. The most popular game for the Jackson Heights kids was auto skiing. It was similar to water skiing, without the skis. Whenever there was enough snow on the ground we would sneak up to the back of a stopped car or bus in the street. We would grab onto the rear bumper and when the vehicle started moving, we would hang on for dear life. The trick was to remain undetected. Many times, when drivers realized what was happening, they would immediately stop, and we would either bang into the car or be forced to let go and fall backward on the hard, icy street. However, most of the time we would just slide along with the car. Sometimes the speeds would be dangerously high, depending on the driver. One time after school I hitched a slide/ride from my elementary school to my house, which was about half a mile. Now that was a good run! We obviously didn't realize how dangerous it was back then. Despite all the madness, I still enjoyed my youth. I was able to go out and do whatever I wanted and go wherever I wanted, as long as I made it home before dark.

I tested my father once and stayed out after dark playing Chinese handball with my friends. He knew where I was and went after me and grabbed me by the ear and dragged me home. My friends were all laughing, yelling, and making fun of me. My dad was no joke, he kept pulling me by the ear the entire way to the apartment. I never stayed out after dark again until I was a teenager.

We would play Chinese handball for hours against a wall on the side of a building on 87th Street, which had commercial storefronts on 37th Avenue. The funny thing is that the actual wall where we played was a Chinese restaurant with the storefront located around the corner. We did not interfere or bother anybody. Back then I had no clue who started the game or where it was from, but now I know that Chinese handball is a form of American handball that was popular on the streets of New York City, Philadelphia, and New Jersey during the 1950s, 60s, 70s, and 80s and is still played today. Different variations are played around the world. Its defining feature is that for a shot to be valid in Chinese or indirect handball, unlike traditional handball, the ball must hit the ground before it hits the wall. We used to play for hours on end. We all became very skilled, and everyone had their specialties. I would like to cut the ball to make it spin erratically. I honestly think that if there was some kind of international competition, we Jackson Heights kids could have won the World Championship. One of the kids had a speed punch serve, other kids had fastball and changeup shots. The game was played with kids lined up on the sidewalk; the actual court was the area of the sidewalk flags or squares, with enough room for about five players. I spent many hours playing with these neighborhood kids. . They were all good athletes. I am sure that the ones who were not sucked into thug life and didn't become casualties of the streets, went on to play team sports for their high schools. It wouldn't surprise me if at least one of them ended up becoming a professional athlete. The volleys were long because everybody was good. It required a lot of sharp hand-eye coordination and reflexes. The balls were hit with a great deal of speed, but with a low trajectory to keep the ball from going out of bounds. It was like sidewalk tennis, except instead of a racket we all used our hands.

As a grown man and a father, I like to win big prizes and stuffed animals at amusement parks and fairs for my kids. The games that require participants to throw oversized balls into tiny holes, utilizing superior hand-eye coordination, require the same skill set that made me an expert at Chinese handball. At a birthday party for my daughter at Adventure Land, a Long Island amusement park, I won stuffed animals for my two daughters and all their friends. I just kept winning and the parents gave me money to win for all the other children. After a while, there were about ten to fifteen little girls walking around the amusement park with giant toy sloths wrapped around their necks. There is something to say about carrying stuffed animal prizes at an amusement park as a badge of honor. I will always cherish that moment; I suppose I will always be a big kid at heart. Today, my wife complains because we have too many stuffed animals in the house. My basement today looks like a toy store such as FAO Schwartz or Toys R Us. Whenever we go to an amusement park, I am forbidden by my wife to play any games. I feel like one of those Las Vegas card counters that are banned from the casinos. Once in a while when we go to an amusement park, I still try to sneak away and win a prize behind my wife's back. I'll pretend to be going to the bathroom or to get some snacks and then I'll come back with giant stuffed animals. I never spend much money because I always win on the first try, thanks to the Chinese handball I played as a kid.

As a child, the best part of summer vacation for me was going to the library. There was no internet, video games or social media back then, so I would escape into books. None of my neighborhood friends knew where I was going; it was my little secret. By the fifth grade I was in what was called the IGC class (Individually Gifted Children). I am sure my neighborhood friends at school wondered why I was not in any of their classes. I was reading and educating myself "on the down low." I loved to read murder mysteries, classics, fiction, non-fiction: I was a voracious reader. I learned about the Mafia and Cosa Nostra before I was old enough to watch classic movies like the *Godfather*, *Good Fellas* and a host of others. From my reading, I felt like I knew all the Mob leaders: Lucky Luciano, Al Capone, Sam Giancana, Paul Castellano, among others. One of John Gotti's sons actually went to high school with my sister years later. It's ironic that during the time I was growing up in Jackson Heights, the Colombian drug cartels, including the Medellin cartel led by Pablo Escobar and the Cali cartel from the same city as my family, began to become powerful. It's ironic that one of the most popular Netflix cable series is *Narcos*, which chronicles the rise of Pablo Escobar and the cartels that gained power and infamy while I was growing up. At that time, Jackson Heights was also called "Little Colombia," because it had the largest Colombian population in the United States. The Colombian drug wars coincided with all the violence and high murder rates found in Jackson Heights in the late 70s and early eighties.

My mom told me that when she was growing up in Cali, when the kids had toothaches, they would chew on the coca leaves that grew wild in Colombia. When my father's cousin Wilfredo would come from Colombia and visit us at our apartment in Jackson Heights, he always acted very suspiciously and looked very nervous. He would visit with his wife, and they were always dressed to the nines: I remember seeing her wearing a mink coat once. Wilfredo insisted that the shades in the apartment should always be closed whenever he visited. I later found out that he was working for the Cali Cartel. Wilfredo ended up getting arrested by the Drug Enforcement Agency and indicted; he lost everything including his wife, who didn't want anything to do with him after he was ruined. The government took all of his money; his assets were confiscated or frozen, and fines were levied. Wilfredo spent a few years in a federal prison on drug trafficking charges. The last time I saw him he was living in a trailer park in Dade County, Florida, with his cousin Carlos – not a very glorious or fairy tale ending. I mention it not as a cautionary tale, but as part of growing up as a First-Generation Colombian.

CHAPTER 4

My parents were not the stereotypical Latino couple. They did not choose to have a lot of kids. Many of our relatives and extended family had up to ten children and/or siblings and even more than that in many cases. The poor Latina mothers ended up being perpetually pregnant throughout their prime years. My parents worked very hard and for long hours, in order to save money so that one day they could get us out of the hood and buy a house in the suburbs. When I would ask for expensive toys or designer clothing, that's what my parents used to tell me. I used to wear hand-me-down clothes when I was a kid, but I was never ashamed, and I tried to make my outfits look cool. I recall wearing my cousin's shiny gold butterfly-collar shirt and polyester suit at a wedding party when that type of clothing was out of style. I looked like John Travolta in *Saturday Night Fever*, but we were then in the early 80s. I thought I looked stylish at the time; I even splashed on my dad's Brut cologne and styled my hair with my mom's Aqua Net hair spray. I put so much hair spray and cologne on that I am surprised my hair did not catch fire, as adults were still smoking a lot back then at parties and events. It may sound embarrassing today but for me it is a fond memory that I will always cherish.

In the mid-70s we moved out of the apartment that we had been sharing with my Tía Diana and her son, my cousin David. We did not go very far: my parents and I moved to another apartment in the same building with my abuelitas, and my Tía

Diana and her son David moved to an apartment on a lower floor. We had to walk down a grand total of one flight of stairs for our many get-togethers at my Tía Diana's. Moving into our own separate apartments was our Latino version of upward mobility. However, over the years my room in our new apartment served as a hotel room for visitors and for relatives that were coming to the United States from Colombia to settle down permanently. I rarely had my new room to myself. My Tía Patty and her son Mateo my mom's cousin Carlos with his two sons Alberto and Edison, my dad's cousin Mary, who stayed with us often, and other extended family and friends who were just visiting New York over the years, all staying in my room for various months at a time. I never complained because I knew we were helping the family. Finally, in 1977, my parents decided to have another baby – a planned event, in contrast to my surprise arrival. My sister, Valeria Ossa, was born on December 25, 1977, in a private hospital in Queens, New York with very little drama.

There was no separate room for my sister, so she slept with my parents until they bought a house six years later. As she got older things became problematic because we all shared one bathroom. We didn't have a car during my early childhood, so for years the whole clan, some twenty or thirty family members and friends, would take the 7 train to the Woodside station and then transfer to the Long Island Railroad (LIRR) to go to the beaches in Long Island. They were not your typical beach trips, and they did not include the typical beach accessories. My family would always bring huge pots and pans, skillets, frying pans, as well as beach wear, coolers, barbecue grills, hammocks, chairs, mini-fridges, water jugs, canteens, umbrellas, meats, vegetables, rice, beans, wine bottles, aguardiente (a typical Colombian drink that translates as "fire water"), water coolers, fishing rods, propane stoves and more items than I can remember. It looked like we were traveling cross country. The only things missing were donkeys, mules, horses and wagons. My dad even carried a machete in a traditional leather sheath, which he could use to cut branches and wood if needed and as protection against any trouble. My father was very protective, and I always felt safe when he was around. He also used to carry a rod that looked like a night stick, which he created at work with fused wires. I don't remember anyone messing with my dad when we were kids. The Long Island Railroad commuters must have been overwhelmed when they saw the entire clan board the train. One characteristic of Latinos, especially my family, is that they tend to be very loud. I miss seeing the faces made by the predominantly Caucasian commuters when they saw us coming.

After my sister was born, my dad bought a vintage Chevrolet Caprice Classic. It was long and brown with a tan top; the air conditioner barely worked and on long trips in the summer we often kept the windows open. What made things extra cozy is that on most trips we would have the entire family squeeze into the two-door sedan. My Tía Diana and my abuelitas were big women, and sometimes we would also wedge in a family friend or two. The driver and two passengers would cram into the front, and five to seven passengers would stuff themselves into the back. We were like a bride trying to squeeze into her wedding dress thirty years later, after having kids. There were no car seats for kids back then, so we would put my sister, little Valeria, in the middle so she wouldn't fly out of a car window. We used to hit our heads on the front seats during sudden stops, or slide and shake around during turns, like clothes in a washing machine or a dryer. Even if there were seatbelts in the back, how could you put seatbelts on that many people in a two-door sedan? My little sister and I would take turns getting car sick and throwing up on long trips. My dad would either have to pull over or we would throw up in plastic bags. I guess it desensitized me because to this day I never get car sick, air sick or seasick. Decades later, I was on a flight with my wife, Sandy and my young daughter, Christina, coming home from a vacation in Mexico. There was a bad storm and the plane kept bouncing and shaking. The turbulence was intense. Everyone on the plane could feel the drops in the pit of their stomachs, as if we were riding a roller coaster. The oxygen masks abruptly came down. Passengers were panicking and screaming. Poor Sandy and Christina were throwing up in the barf bags. I was completely calm and feeling fresh and cool as a cucumber. My childhood trips toughened me up, but I wouldn't recommend that type of therapy to anyone.

    My dad enjoyed the outdoors and loved to swim. After he bought that used car, we were always going to beaches in Long Island and New Jersey or to lakes and rivers in upstate New York and Connecticut, and to many other places. My dad taught us how to swim at an early age. It was a source of pride for my father that we were all strong swimmers, capable of swimming way out into a lake or river. My sister competed on both her junior high and high school swim teams. I completed lifeguard training and competed in a mile-long swimming competition. Many years later my wife and my two daughters, Christina and Lili, were hanging out with my sister at Rockaway Beach in Far Rockaway. I was working long hours as an attorney at the time and could not be there. The water and the tides were rough that day. My wife got caught in the undertow and was sucked into the ocean. My sister immediately sprang into action when she realized that Sandy was in trouble and ran into the water, swam out, grabbed her and brought her safely back to shore. My wife said that she was swallowing water and felt like she was going to drown.

My dad's favorite place to go was Wildwood State Park, located in Riverhead, New York. The beach was very rocky, but the water was somewhat clear (for New York, not like the Bahamas or Cancun) and tranquil. Every time we went my dad would say that one day, we would all swim out to a large rock that looked like a small island in the ocean. It was very far out, probably about half a mile or three-quarters of a mile from the shore. When my sister was finally old enough and my dad was still young enough, we decided to attempt to swim out to the rock. It was early in the morning. It was a long and arduous swim, and it seemed like we were swimming forever. There were no lifeguards or tourists in that section of the beach, only fishermen. My mom and abuelitas were at the picnic area, which was about a mile from the beach, so they had no idea what was happening. As we were swimming toward the rock, I saw a lot of fish swimming by me. When I saw some sharks, I wanted to swim back, but we had gone so far that there was no turning back. Of the three of us, I was probably the fittest because I was a teenager, and my sister was young at the time. I am sure my dad and my sister didn't even notice the sharks because they were working so hard just to make it to the rock. Once we all made it, we held on to that rock for dear life. I felt like we had just climbed Mount Everest! I wish waterproof sports cameras had been available at that time. We could have taken a memorable picture. We were on such an adrenaline rush and felt such a sense of euphoria that swimming back to shore was a breeze. I don't think my father, sister and I ever felt closer. To this day I remember that moment with a great sense of pride. If my mom had found out what we did that day she would have killed my dad.

My father was obsessed with getting to the beach as early as humanly possible. If we were going to the beach, the family would all have to get up at the crack of dawn so that we could beat the traffic and secure a good spot at the picnic area. Most of our extended family and friends showed up late, but there were always prime picnic tables waiting for them. My mom, my abuelitas, my sister and I were all half asleep on most of our family excursions to the beach. My dad was like a drill sergeant. My mom would say, "Tony, do we really have to leave this early?" It was like a comedy routine because he would never listen. He was too focused on putting everything in the trunk and getting an early start. On a typical Sunday morning in the hood, club and party goers would be coming home from places like Studio 54, Palladium, or the Sound Factory and the Ossa family would be gearing up to go to the beach. The drunks would be passed out or lying around in the bushes by our building; the ladies of the night would be finishing their shifts. I wish I had owned a video camera then so I could record all the madness and the reactions of the old neighborhood characters to the Ossas heading out to the beach. I remember always hearing a lot of snickering and laughter. The Ossas would always leave before the sun came up.

When we arrived at Wildwood State Park we would not even have to pay to get in because technically the park was still closed, and the toll booth clerk would not start his shift for hours. I remember seeing wildlife at the picnic area when we were unloading the car. I saw deer, snakes, rabbits, opossums, squirrels, raccoons, and many other interesting creatures. They were still feasting at their buffet: the scraps from the picnic goers from the previous day. They did not expect the humans to arrive so early. Even the wildlife was mad at my dad. I remember seeing an owl once. It was cool, because the only owl I had ever seen was the Tootsie Roll cartoon owl from the commercials on TV. Owls are beautiful and majestic animals; however, I could have gone to the zoo in the afternoon to see one; I didn't have to see a real owl for the first time at an ungodly hour on a Sunday morning!

Wildwood State Park became like a second home to the Ossa family.

My dad even started taking us camping at the park's campground. In 1979, on a father-son bonding trip on Labor Day weekend, my father and I set up camp as Hurricane David was storming toward New York. My dad ignored the warnings and explained that the media and the weathermen were exaggerating and were always wrong. His favorite saying was *"va a escampar,"* which translates as the weather will clear up. Hurricane David went down in history as a deadly hurricane that caused death and destruction in the Caribbean, Florida and on the Atlantic coast, including New York. David was believed to have been responsible for thousands of deaths, making it one of the deadliest hurricanes in the modern era. My father was wrong again when it came to his optimistic weather predictions and the storm hit Long Island with a vengeance. We woke up one morning in our tent at the campsite and heard howling winds and a torrential downpour. Water was leaking into our tent and my sleeping bag was soaked. When we got up and looked outside there were tents flying around all over the place. The campers were all running and driving away in droves; it was like a disaster movie. Branches, leaves, propane stoves, sleeping bags, tarps, tents, tent poles and assorted items were flying everywhere like projectile missiles. My dad finally gave in and said, "I guess it's not going to clear up." We packed up quickly and drove away from the campsite like bats out of hell. My dad was laughing on the ride home and winked at me and said, "Don't tell your mother." My mother was visiting family in Colombia at the time, and I never did tell her. The Ossas had a habit of keeping secrets from each other over the years.

One of my favorite memories is diving for mussels in the ocean at Wildwood. Early in the morning when the tide was low, I could swim out and pick mussels from the bottom of the ocean. I felt like a commercial diver or a fisherman. My dad would bring buckets and we would fill them up. While I picked the mussels our family friends would fish for porgy, blue fish and striped bass, which were in abundance back then. By the time we finished, we would have a large haul, more than enough to feed everyone at the picnic area. Back then my mom's cousin Jaime would prepare all the fish and mussels. To add flavor, he would put all the mussels in a lemon broth that he had prepared. Those mussels were delicious, and I felt so proud that my family and friends were eating from the fruits of my labor. Jaime was a great cook and he enjoyed preparing many different gourmet meals, including a seasoned rabbit dish that was tasty but not my cup of tea. He would prepare morcilla (blood sausage), chunchullo on the grill (beef intestines), lengua (cow tongue) and even shark stew. Latinos love to eat non-traditional foods, but I was grateful that we also had grilled chicken and steak.

My dad was very adventurous, so one weekend he decided we would go somewhere new: Fire Island, which he heard had beautiful beaches. So we drove to a ferry out on Long Island and headed to Fire Island, but we ended up at Cherry Grove. Fire Island and Cherry Grove were and still are considered two of the most popular LGBTQ-welcoming resorts and beaches. That day, only my immediate family went on that trip to Fire Island, including my parents, abuelitas, Tía Diana my little sister Valeria and me. I noticed when we were on the ferry that there were a lot of men looking at us as if we were aliens (not illegal aliens but actual aliens from outer space). I remember seeing a lot of smirks and funny looks. When we arrived at the beach there was no picnic area. We carved out a small picnic area in a corner of the beach, including portable tables, a propane stove, beach chairs, blankets and of course pots and pans. We were going to have sancocho, a traditional, hearty Colombian soup filled with meat, potatoes, yucca and vegetables. As we set up, I saw a man jog by us wearing nothing more than a head band. That's when we figured out that it was a nude-optional beach. I remember my Abuelita Hortencia, well into her seventies, was staring at him hard. I thought that she was going to get up and chase after him. I never thought about my abuelita as being sexual, although she did outlive two husbands in Colombia.

My dad was so stubborn that instead of realizing that we should leave, he insisted that the beach was beautiful and that we were having an exciting new adventure. Valeria was young, so she probably does not remember any of what went on that day. My mom told my dad that we should leave but he refused to listen. It's notable that all those gay men never said a word to us or made us feel unwelcome. I remember seeing men holding hands, kissing and being intimate for the first time in my life. In those days it was taboo to be gay but at Fire Island gay men could just be happy and be comfortable in their own skins. I felt like we were invisible because no one said a word about the crazy Latino family hanging out at the beach. We were the outsiders and everyone else was comfortable and felt at home. I know that society frowned on homosexuality at that time, but I just remember seeing people feeling comfortable and being themselves. Today, I love to listen to a famous Radio DJ, Elvis Duran, who has a popular morning show in New York City. He has a guest on his show, Uncle Johnny, who has served as a bartender and is a gay celebrity at Cherry's on the Bay at Cherry Grove on Fire Island. Uncle Johnny would have been working that day. I wonder if he remembers seeing a crazy family that brought their grandmas and kids to Cherry Grove for a day at the beach.

CHAPTER 5

The AIDS epidemic in the '80s hit the Latino community hard, although the HIV virus affected people of all races and ethnicities. In the beginning, the media portrayed HIV to be a predominantly gay disease, and the gay community was unfairly vilified by the media. Later it was established that it was a disease transmitted through intravenous drug use and unprotected sex. I believe that the AIDS epidemic affected First-Generation Latinos more than any other ethnic group. Many young Latinos immigrated to the United States in the late 60s and early 70s. In most Latino countries back then young men and women could not be openly gay. Many young men and women who were leading double lives or hiding their sexuality were scared to be disowned by their families or even attacked and ostracized by the communities where they had been raised. During the '60s and '70s, Latin America was inflexible when it came to acceptance or even tolerance of the gay community. Rather than coming out and trying to find happiness, Latinos were forced to have secret relationships. Sadly, there were cases of disenchanted gay Latinos that could no longer live the charade and resorted to committing suicide. Young gay Latinos who came to the United States, especially to New York City and San Francisco, felt liberated and were finally able to have active social lives and feel comfortable in their own skins. Latin America was and still is extremely conservative when it comes to religion and homosexuality. In the United States, white radical far-right conservatives and hate groups, especially those ultra-conservative members of historic hate organizations, believe that many Latinos are heathens and are part of an inferior race. The irony is that old-school Latino immigrants have something in common with these hate groups when it comes to attitudes about freedom of expression and sexuality. Many Latinos still believe that homosexuality is a choice and that same-sex relationships are an affront to God. Some teenagers cannot even come out to their own grandparents, who will never understand or comprehend.

My mother's cousin Jaime was an integral part of my family and our lives. He came to the United States around the same time that my parents met. He also lived in Jackson Heights, about half a mile from where I grew up. Jaime and his partner, Alfredo, were a couple, and openly gay. Jaime was short, dark-skinned and chubby; he had straight hair, which according to many Latinos is the same as "good hair." My family would tell me that the color of a person's skin was not as important as whether they had "good" or "bad" hair. Of course, this is all preposterous. You get into these debates with all types of cultures and ethnic groups. There is a famous singer, Beyoncé, who in an R&B lyric from a song called "Lemonade" refers to her famous rapper husband Jay Z's paramour as "Becky with the good hair." In many Latino communities there are mothers and grandmothers that still preach to their children, "Make sure you marry someone with 'good hair'." It's disappointing that even as an historically oppressed people, some old-school Latinos help to perpetuate negative stereotypes.

Jaime's lover Alfredo was from Uruguay. He was a tall, handsome man with silver hair, pale white skin, and deep blue eyes. If you did not know that he was Latino, you would think he was German or Austrian, certainly of European descent. We know the rumors about Germans, Austrians and Nazi war criminals going to South America after World War II, but I never thought about who Alfredo's parents could have been. I just knew him as Jaime's partner. They seemed very happy together and were always caring and kind to me. I considered Alfredo as part of the family, and Jaime and Alfredo were part of the beach crew. Wherever we went, Alfredo would always fish and bring back all kinds of delicacies for everyone to enjoy, including bass, blue fish, porgy, trout and many other delicious fish. He had a knack for catching them, and all the other fishermen would be jealous. When white American fishermen would ask him what his secret was, he spoke to them in broken English with a heavy Spanish accent. They were always shocked at his accent because of the way he looked. I remember some ignorant fisherman saying, "Damn, that guy is a *spic*!" The moral of the story is that Latinos come in many different colors, sizes and shapes.

Jaime and Alfredo enjoyed life to the fullest and always seemed to be happy and inseparable. I have fond memories of all the get-togethers with Jaime and Alfredo. Latinos are constantly finding an excuse to have a get-together or a house party, and it seemed like most of the house parties back then were at Jaime and Alfredo's place, including for baptisms, first communions, confirmations, and marriages. No one could afford to rent a hall or have elaborate receptions at fancy catering places; however, the parties and celebrations were always a collaborative effort, and all the families would bring different dishes and desserts. It was like a potluck with restaurant-quality food; there was always more than enough to eat and everyone would have leftovers to take home. Jaime was a great cook and between his cooking, our family friends' cooking and my abuelitas' cooking, it was always an embarrassment of riches. Paella, arroz con pollo, steak and chicken seasoned to perfection, ropa vieja, ensaladas, shrimp, lobster, tamales, fish, tostones, empanadas, the obligatory rice and beans, pernil, arepas, arroz con leche that melted in your mouth, and all types of traditional cakes and pastries. There was traditional Colombian food, Argentinian food, Uruguayan food, Puerto Rican food, Cuban food and even more. It was like a cooking competition, but the winners were the guests.

The music was always traditional Latino music, including plenty of salsa, merengue, cumbia, and bolero. The living room was cleared out and transformed into a dance floor with an elaborate portable vinyl floor that rivaled the famed Copa Cabana night club. Furniture would be temporarily placed in the hallway outside of the apartment, certainly in violation of the fire codes. Guests of all ages – from toddlers to senior citizens – would dance for hours. The best dancers were often the older folks. Sometimes I felt intimidated by their expert dance moves, and I would hang out in a bedroom with the other kids. To this day some of the best dancers I have seen in my life were at those house parties; they could even be favorably compared to professional dancers. I didn't know I was a good dancer until I was a young adult and I started going to American house parties and clubs. When I got married the guests at the wedding reception were a mixture of my wife's and my immigrant and traditional family friends. We also invited our new friends from work and our new Caucasian friends and their families from the suburbs. The wedding video tells it all. We had to push for multiple conga lines to get everyone involved because many of the guests were intimidated by all the great dancers and refused to get on the dance floor.

In the mid-80s Jaime suddenly became sick. I would see him

from time to time and he always looked very pale and gaunt. The last time I saw poor Jaime he was a shell of himself and literally was down to skin and bones. Jaime was only in his mid-forties. My parents told me that he had some type of cancer, but I later found out that he was HIV positive and had contracted AIDS. The AIDS epidemic was still in its early stages before all of the research and medical advancements. At that time, when someone was diagnosed with HIV it was equivalent to a death sentence. The parties and the get-togethers came to a screeching halt. In some ways, I believe that it was also the end of my innocence. Jaime died a few years later, while it was still early in the epidemic and there was a lot of ignorance due to a lack of education regarding HIV and AIDS. Jaime was cremated because at that time, unfortunately, it was against the law in New York for individuals who died of AIDS to be buried in a cemetery. Jaime grew up as a devout Catholic, despite the Catholic Church's official stance about his lifestyle. He was the friendliest, most loving male adult relative I knew then, and he would give the shirt off his back to help anyone in need. It was the first time that someone really close to me had died. After he passed away, I felt that a small part of me died with him.

  Jaime contracted HIV because his partner and lover of many years, Alfredo, had flings with younger men. Before the AIDS epidemic, times were radically different. In the '60s and '70s, we had Woodstock, clubs like Studio 54 or Plato's Retreat, and the sexual revolution. The world was different and carefree. Alfredo died of AIDS-related complications years later. There were a lot of great people that we loved who died of AIDS during the '80s, such as Freddy Mercury, Rock Hudson and so many others. When heterosexual celebrities began contracting HIV, the media and the world finally came to the realization that it was not just a gay disease. I remember when EZ E, of the groundbreaking Gangsta rap group NWA, came forward and admitted that he was HIV positive. He died too soon. I enjoyed his music and later learned to appreciate him even more. So many others died from intravenous drug use and unprotected sex. Many Latinos were doing heroin back then. Addiction killed many members of minority groups and people of color in the '80s. When Earvin Magic Johnson, the greatest point guard in the history of the NBA and a superstar with the Los Angeles Lakers, held a press conference and admitted that he was HIV positive it seemed like the world was coming to an end. He was a hero to so many people including sports fans around the world and the African American community. The world finally realized that AIDS was not just a gay disease and more resources were allotted to create new advances in medicine, so the HIV virus was eventually contained and was no longer a death sentence. Thirty years later, Earvin Magic Johnson is still alive and healthy, and he continues to be a sports icon and a pillar in the African American community through his various business ventures. He is still loved by the world regardless of his skin color and his HIV diagnosis.

As I am completing this book, the COVID-19 pandemic is hitting the world hard, with unprecedented death and destruction. We cannot blame one group based on sexual preference, religion or ethnicity. It is irresponsible to give up and point to the end of days. All religions have scriptures that refer to the end of the world as we know it. As history has taught us, we shall overcome. I would argue that we have been overcoming social injustice, widespread disease and pandemics and unnecessary wars and genocide for thousands of years.

When I was a young boy, my cousin Mateo came to the United States to make a better life for himself. He was in his early twenties, and he stayed with us for a few years back in Jackson Heights at Hotel Ossa – i.e., my room. It was the late 70s and early 80s and he immersed himself in the culture. He loved disco music and introduced me to the famous artist Donna Summer, the Queen of Disco. He used to play her albums all the time, back then when people were still listening to vinyl records. The gay community loved her. My cousin Mateo was gay, but he never said anything to my family. I think they knew, but they never criticized him for anything. He worked two or three jobs at a time and was trying to save enough money to bring his mother, my Tía Patty and his sister Laura to the United States from Colombia. He was always friendly, caring and kind to me, and very respectful to my family. He took English classes at night and always pushed me to speak to him in English so he could learn. Through hard work, blood, sweat and tears, Mateo became a partner in a carpet-cleaning business and was able to move out of my parents' apartment and get his own place after only a year. I looked up to him and was proud of him. I found out that he was gay because I accidentally overheard a phone conversation, he had with one of his boyfriends. It did not change my opinion of him. I spoke to my mother about it and she told me that everyone is different when they're born, and everyone is entitled to be happy. Even though homosexuality had a very negative stigma at that time, what my mother said made sense to me and I didn't care about what anybody thought – I loved Mateo. He was my cousin and he worked hard to make it in the United States, the old-fashioned way.

    Mateo finally saved enough money to bring his mother and sister to the United States from Colombia. My Tía Patty and cousin Laura stayed at hotel Ossa for a little while. When Mateo met an older Caucasian man named Henry, they fell in love and lived together for many years. Unfortunately, Henry did not know that he was already HIV positive when they first met, and Henry and Mateo both became sick. Henry was wealthy and owned property, and he bequeathed all his belongings to Mateo in his will before he died. Henry's family had disowned him many years earlier, when he came out of the closet. Poor Mateo did not die quickly, and he suffered for many years; this was before HIV was manageable and not a death sentence. As a teenager, I already had my learner's permit and my parents allowed me to drive Mateo to his medical appointments after his health deteriorated so quickly that he could no longer drive himself. His mother and sister had to work to support themselves.

What I remember most was that he was still young, but his hair had turned prematurely gray. He was in constant pain because he hated taking the morphine and opioids that he was prescribed for the pain. He would moan and groan and often cry. He was very apologetic because he worried that he was making me feel uncomfortable, but I told him that he should just act in any way that made him feel comfortable. He was very graphic in his descriptions of his suffering and what he was feeling at times, but I did not care because I knew he was dying, and I wanted him to feel free and let it all out. Toward the end, I no longer recognized my vibrant, young, hip cousin that I met years earlier. It was hard for me to deal with, but it made me feel good that I could help my family. I even took school days off to help him out. My Tía Patty had tears in her eyes when I brought him home after the many trips to the doctor's office. I wish I could have done more.

Mateo died, but his legacy will live on forever. Patty was able to buy a house in Forest Hills Queens with the inheritance money that her son left her. It was a beautiful house in a middle-class neighborhood. Her daughter was able to be reunited with her fiancé Leo, who came from Colombia. Years later they sold that house and moved to Florida. Today they live near Fort Lauderdale in a beautiful house. Laura married Leo and they had two lovely girls, Victoria and Lily. Patty met a good man named Pedro, and they have been together for many years. Today they all live together in that house, and I like to imagine that Mateo is smiling in heaven, waiting to be reunited with his family one day.

CHAPTER 6

Back in 1980, my fifth-grade elementary school teacher, Ms. Infanti, had the entire class take IQ tests as part of a recruiting effort by St. John's University for their program designed for gifted children. I am grateful to Ms. Infanti for her progressive ideas. I felt privileged to be one of just two students in my class who were accepted into the program, and I was the only one who attended. Some of my favorite childhood memories are of going to St. John's University on Saturday mornings. The classes were held at the college campus, which made me feel like a college student. I had never seen a college campus before then. There were majestic buildings, large expanses of grass and gates around the campus; it looked like a small city. I felt proud to be able to walk those college grounds. The kid who lived and grew up next to the 7 Train on Roosevelt Avenue in the hood was a college man walking on what felt like hallowed grounds. There are many beautiful campuses around the United States that are much bigger and more beautiful, especially Ivy League schools like Harvard and Yale, or famous schools known for their sports programs and academics such as Kentucky, Michigan, North Carolina, Stanford, etc. However, at that time I could not imagine anything looking more perfect than the St. John's University campus. This experience had a profound influence on my life, as I decided to go to St. John's Law School when I was older. As part of the Gifted Children Program, I took a law and government class and a communications class. It was fun meeting kids that were smart and were working hard. I never hung out with any overachievers back in the old neighborhood. After taking those two classes, I thought about becoming a lawyer or an actor. I could not believe that I was finally thinking beyond my circumstances and broadening my horizons. I would have loved to become an actor, but who knows what would have happened. Perhaps I would be waiting tables or working as a bartender, looking for small parts in TV shows and commercials. I ultimately chose law, and it has been an interesting and fulfilling career.

After I was accepted into the gifted children's program, my dad believed that I was a prodigy who was going to attend Harvard University. I honestly don't know what he was thinking, putting that much pressure on a ten-year-old boy who grew up in the hood. As part of my communications class at St. John's, we all had to create a news skit like the iconic *Saturday Night Live* weekend update segment. My plan was to show how the bad neighborhoods in New York City were improving and to mention that crime was at an all-time low. At that time the exact opposite was true, since crime was at an all-time high. In the '80s, there was no Google so other than the rough neighborhood where I was raised, I had no idea about what other tough neighborhoods existed. I asked my dad and he mentioned a few, including Bushwick, East New York, Brownsville, Bedford-Stuyvesant, Spanish Harlem and the South Bronx, among others. I only knew about my hood, but I took his word for it. When we taped the newscast in class, I had a segment as a correspondent: the camera turned to me and I discussed how New York City was changing for the better. I claimed that the historically bad crime and murder rates in all these neighborhoods were at an all-time low. (Ironically, in the future many of these neighborhoods would become gentrified and hip, and thus desirable places to live.)

During the broadcast, as I discussed the decrease in crime, I was shot and killed. We used sound effects, and I had fake prop blood come out of my mouth and pretended to die. Throughout the rest of the broadcast, I remained dead, slumped in a chair at the news desk with my head down. I wish that I had the footage, but just like many aspects of my youth, it disappeared and cannot be recovered.

Ms. Infanti used to teach us how to meditate and brainstorm. Being a young Latino kid, this was all strange to me. She pushed us to excel, and she expanded our horizons. We had so many talented students in our class that we used to put on plays and other performances for the entire school. I choreographed the fifth-grade school play. I incorporated skits that I knew from my Boy Scout experiences and worked out other ideas with the class. We all collaborated on the costumes with the help of Ms. Infanti and the parents. Our fancy costumes made us feel like we were part of a professional Broadway production. The 5th Grade play was such a success that we received standing ovations and the school allowed for encore performances so other neighboring schools could attend. Ms. Infanti, my favorite teacher to this day, told me that she knew that I would be a successful actor or producer one day. When I told my dad, he looked at me sternly and said *"Pa' qué va a hacer eso?"* which translates as "Why are you going to waste your time like that?" Sadly, my parents never saw any of my performances because they could not take time off work.

Ms. Infanti set goals for us minority kids and did not make us feel like we were inferior. I thought that the IQ test was unfair because there were questions about global studies and US history and current events that I knew that anybody that I grew up with would not be able to answer. I question the validity of measuring someone's intelligence by their knowledge of current events or US and global history. The Incas, Mayans and Aztecs were Latin American indigenous civilizations whose great achievements are often not included in the curriculum in US schools despite being advanced civilizations that made countless contributions to the modern world. I scored high on the IQ test because I used to read a lot when I was a kid. Not everybody has that privilege.

I received good grades throughout elementary school without even trying. The worst part of elementary school was when my teachers would send letters to my house for not completing homework assignments. Some of the assignments were so simple that I was too bored to do them, but I was always doing well on my exams. My dad did not care. So, every time that a letter came home, he would punish me, but not with a "time out," as many American parents do. He would make me take off my pants and then he hit me with the belt repeatedly. Usually, he would hit me until I cried hysterically or until he drew blood. When he was a kid in Colombia his dad would hit him with a whip or make him walk on his knees on raw rice. There is an old-school population out there that defends these actions by alleging that corporal punishment works and the problem with our youth today is that they are coddled and spoiled. My daughters are both honor students and anyone who lays a hand on them will answer to me. My dad kept beating me as a form of punishment until I was a teenager. One day I told him that if he hit me again, I would hit him back. That's when it stopped. I still feel bad for saying that to my own father. I love my dad, but I was young and angry, and I honestly felt that I was capable of beating him the way he beat me when I was growing up. I vowed that if I had children, they would never be exposed to that kind of punishment.

By the end of elementary school, I knew that I was going to

a newly formed magnet school. Ms. Infanti had everyone in the class apply; she liked to push the envelope and expose us to new experiences. I was accepted to IS 227, the Louis Armstrong School, founded in 1979 as a court-ordered experiment in racial integration. Louis Armstrong represented the philosophy that children learn best when they have classmates from different ethnic groups, neighborhoods, and academic abilities. It was an experimental school that brought together urban kids from different cultures and different neighborhoods. The Louis Armstrong Middle School mission statement was to bring together a group of culturally diverse children to help them grow academically, emotionally, physically, and socially.

Generally, people have awful memories of middle school. They were either bullied or felt like they did not fit in. I believe that you could ask any student from my graduation year, and they would tell you the same thing. However, I loved the Louis Armstrong School because it was a great learning experience that broadened my horizons and exposed me to new cultures and friends. I had never met so many kids from so many different cultures. I was always hardcore Latino because that's all I knew, but at IS 227, for the first time I made friends with young people who were Irish, Italian, Black, Asian, Arabic and Jewish. We discovered that we had the same hopes, dreams and ambitions and we had more in common than we had previously thought. One of my best friends in the sixth grade was Chris Jackson and he was Black. When I invited him to my house for the first time my parents scolded me. That's when I found out that my parents were not as opened-minded as I am. They told me that we were from different cultures and that Blacks and Latinos were like oil and water. They did not forbid me to be friends with him but discouraged me from inviting him over again. They explained that I would understand when I got older. I am older now, but I still don't understand them because I learned very early in life that racism is ugly and I shouldn't judge anyone by the color of their skin. My dad bought me an Atari video game which was old-fashioned compared to the video game systems that followed, but I enjoyed playing. I would invite Chris over with his cousins and we would hang out and play video games for hours. I think that my parents were the ones who didn't understand, and I had it right all along.

My best friend at IS 227 was Raf, a First-Generation Latino like me. When I first met him, I thought he was kind of nerdy; however, I learned quickly that he was super smart, but never acted like it. He was always humble and never acted like he was better than anyone. Raf and I became great friends because I was the Ying to his Yang. Raf grew up in a strict religious household with his Christian mother and grandmother. I think that I was the right friend to encourage his creative side. He used to come over to my apartment and we would listen to hip records that my cousin Mateo had left for me. Mateo was a DJ in Colombia and loved music. I got Raf hip to this old cool song, "Jungle Fever," which rose to number eight on the Billboard Hot 100 in 1972. It went like this: "*Ay, ay, qué fiebre, así, así, ay qué fiebre.*" There was heavy breathing and moaning with sexual overtones. It was an underground cult classic and perfect for two Latino teenagers with strict parents.

I invited my buddy Raf on a camping trip with my family at Wildwood State Park in Riverhead Long Island. The park had everything you could imagine. There was a beautiful beach, even though it was a little rocky, but the water was calm and clear in comparison to other Long Island beaches. There were also basketball courts, hills, trails, trees, wildlife and plenty of room to explore. There were even camping grounds in the park where families would pitch tents and camp out for the weekends or for weeks at a time during the summer. While the parents pretended to know what they were doing, like true outdoorsmen and women, the kids would play. There were always city slickers pretending to love the outdoors, with plenty of miserable kids looking for ways to have fun. Imagine kids today with no iPads, iPods, iPhones, smartphones, Apple watches, tablets, computers, or laptops; oh no, they would want to declare a state of emergency! This trip might be considered cruel and unusual punishment by kids today.

It was the summer of 1982 and Raf and I had just finished the seventh grade. Our hormones were out of control and puberty was hitting us hard. We made friends with a group of kids at the campsite, and we were invited to a late-night, secret party at the beach. I knew that if I asked for permission, my dad would not let us go because he was so strict. So that evening after dinner I told my dad that we were going for a walk and that we would be right back.

He replied, "Don't go too far and make sure you and your friend are back soon – it's getting late."

Raf looked nervous but I gave him a wink as if to say, "Don't worry, I got this covered." In the calmest, most innocent voice I could muster, I told my dad, "Of course, Papi, you know me." I knew that we would be in trouble when we got back but it was worth the risk. In the business, insurance, and legal worlds and in many other fields it is called a risk-benefit analysis. We were two horny teens, and, at that age, the benefits far outweighed the risks. We did not need any advanced degrees to figure that one out. There were so many cute girls who also snuck away and a bunch of us got together at the beach and played spin the bottle underneath the stars. The game involved kids sitting in a circle with a bottle in the middle and each player would spin. Whoever it landed on had to kiss whoever spun it. It was dark out and most of us knew that we would be punished, but it was worth it. I had never kissed so many pretty girls in my young life. We were having so much fun, but our game came to an abrupt halt when all the parents, who had formed a giant search-and-rescue party, finally found us.

Could you imagine a bunch of parents walking around the campsite looking for their knucklehead kids that night? The conversations went something like this:

"Have you seen my little Jill?"

"No, have you seen my Jack?"

Suddenly all the parents are asking their camping neighbors the same thing. "Little Johnny told me he was going for a walk."

"That's what my Jane told me."

"What?"

I wonder how long it took them to figure it out. They probably kept bumping into each other for hours and finally realized that we must be hanging out together. The parents in the search party were all walking around with flashlights and some of them even had canteens. Some of the dads looked like Indiana Jones looking for lost treasure. I could have sworn somebody was carrying a flaming torch. Did they think we had been abducted? Did they think we were being held captive in a cave somewhere? No, we were just a bunch of horny teens having fun! When the parents found us and saw that we were safe and just having fun, they were very relieved.

Most of the parents were understanding and I overheard a

few dads – probably the ones that had sons and not the ones that had daughters – saying "teenagers will be teenagers." Today I have two young daughters and I am as open-minded as anyone, but not sure I would have the same reaction. Talk about being a hypocrite and having double standards. Oh well, I grew up to be a Latino father after all. A lot of the parents and kids went back to the campsites joking around and laughing together like it was a fun adventure. My dad was old-school, and he did not say anything to me or Raf when he first saw us. It was dark out, but I could see the smoke coming out of his ears like boiling water escaping from a tea kettle. My dad just grabbed us both by the ears, one ear with each hand. He didn't say a word and walked us the mile or so from the beach back to the campsite. I felt bad for Raf, but my dad did not care, he was hardcore that way. With apologies to Raf, I have to admit that it was worth it!

The next year as seniors at the Louis Armstrong School, Raf and I and my crew all felt like we ruled the school in the eighth grade. Carlito, who had been my friend since the sixth grade, was now considered cool. A lot of us kids sprouted between seventh and eighth grade. Carlito had a big afro and always took immaculate care of his sneakers and his "fro." His mom was Latina, and his father was Black, but to me he was just a good friend. I never did ask him which ethnicity he identified most with, but I am sure America saw him only as Black back in the early 80s. I never met anyone that kept his sneakers in such immaculate shape. Everyone who was anyone was wearing Pumas and Adidas shell-top sneakers, with the thick laces. Carlito carried a toothbrush with him to brush his sneakers whenever they would get dirty or if somebody stepped on them. His fro was always so perfect and pristine. As a Latino my hair was different, but that fro was a work of art. Carlito taught me how to hook up my laces on my sneakers so that the lace design would start small on the bottom and get wider as you went up. Some kids intertwined different color laces to make designs like checkers. The trick was to stuff the sneakers before you laced them up. I used to use tennis balls, so the sneaker was expanded while you were putting on the laces. You had to buy the special thick laces that were very popular and were sold everywhere in the hood. I remember old-school graffiti murals and characters wearing Pumas or Adidas with thick, colored laces. The only problem was that in order to look cool you could not actually tie the sneakers, so you felt like you were walking with slippers on. Whenever we played sports at recess – handball, punchball, basketball or football – my sneakers would fly off my feet all the time. I had to start wearing extra socks, since I preferred having sweaty feet to wearing sneakers in the traditional way.

During a parent-teacher conference, my social studies teacher told my parents that I was a great student, but I had to be careful with the way I dressed, including my sneakers and with the friends that I chose. I wish the teacher had left the parenting to the parents. I was hit with the belt when we got home that night, due to those pearls of wisdom. I used to like to wear sweatshirts with logos and designs on the front and letters on the side or back. Many neighborhood crews would wear these sweatshirts like uniforms. At that time, the CC Boys and Rockers Revenge were the popular crews in the neighborhood. These sweatshirts would be custom made at the local shops. I had a sweatshirt made with a design of marijuana leaves in a marijuana field that said, "And on the eighth day God created Colombia." Not one of my proudest moments as a Colombian American. I just thought the shirt looked cool. Perhaps my social studies teacher had a point. One Sunday morning I was going to church with my parents like all good Catholic Latino kids did, and I wore that shirt. I just grabbed it because it was clean, and I was half-asleep as we would always go to the early mass. I don't think my parents had noticed what was on that sweatshirt. When my mom looked at my sweatshirt before we left for church, she started screaming hysterically and told me to take it off. My dad gave me the death stare and I knew that I had to change. As our family walked down the building stairs that day, two degenerate kids were smoking weed in the stairwell on the first floor (on a Sunday morning!). I looked at my mom and her face turned beet red and I could see the steam coming out of her ears. I secretly wanted to say: "See, Mom, it's natural – everyone is doing it." I'm glad I kept quiet because she was so angry that she might have killed me!

My mom was still mad because that summer I came up with this crazy idea to visit her at work with my neighborhood friend Greg. We were just looking for money, and the plan was to take the subway to the financial district in New York City. My mom worked at the Citibank corporate headquarters located on Water Street in the Wall Street area. It was hot out, so Greg and I were wearing shorts, sneakers, and T-shirts. I took off my shirt and tied it around my waist, while Greg took off his and tied it around his head like a do-rag or a skull cap. We looked like we were at the park playing a basketball game with teams of shirts and skins. On the subway, we received a lot of dirty looks from business types in suits and a lot of staring and when we arrived at the Citibank building a security guard accosted us immediately. He yelled into his walkie talkie and a bunch of other guards showed up.

Trying to show off in front of my friend, I became

belligerent: "Yo, get off me, my mom works here – Carmen Ossa!" I refused to leave, so one of the guards finally reached out to the front desk and had my mother paged. When she arrived at the front door and saw my friend and me shirtless, surrounded by security guards, I knew we had made a big mistake. I had never visited her at work. She was shocked to see us, and she wondered how we got there and how I knew the building where she worked. When I was younger, she took me to see a Christmas show they put on for employees and their families, and I remembered the building. She didn't know that I already knew how to take the subway. If looks could kill, I wouldn't be writing this now. She grabbed my friend and me by the arms, dragged us outside, threw some money at me, then told us to go home immediately and never come back dressed like that. She said that she wasn't going to tell my dad because she knew what he would do to me, and she kept her word. I loved my mom and I felt terrible about embarrassing her, but luckily none of her coworkers saw anything. When she got home after work, she advised me not to do that again because it was dangerous riding the trains unsupervised at my age. After apologizing to her, I cried because I hated letting my mom down. She gave me a kiss and hugged me and told me that no matter what I did, she would always love me. My father never found out, but if he had, he would have moved us out of the neighborhood that fall.

There were shops in the old neighborhood that used to sell all kinds of drug paraphernalia like bongs, bamboo paper, scales and so forth. They would also customize and sell T-shirts, sweatshirts, belts, and other clothing, as well as many cool items like inexpensive jewelry, that were popular at the time. I bought a black leather belt there, with a giant gold-plated buckle with my name on it. Some kids had nicknames put on the buckles, and sometimes they would lie and say that the buckles were made of solid gold. Of course, the belts were not worn for comfort. You did not tighten the belt, but let it hang down so that everyone could see the gold-plated buckle. A lot of kids wore shorts underneath their jeans so that when their pants dropped down below their waist with the loose belts, they would not be exposing their butt cheeks. Inner-city kids still wear loose-fitting pants and shorts today. It seems like over the years the pants got looser and baggier to the point that you see kids wearing jeans that go down almost to their knees. Back then kids used to like to wear Lee jeans that came in a variety of colors, just like the popular candy brands Jaw Breakers or Skittles, and you could color-coordinate with all your sneakers and customized sweatshirts and T-shirts. A popular kind of hat at the time was the Kangol, worn by the famous LL Cool J, who was from a neighborhood in the borough of Queens, called Jamaica. I could not rock a Kangol, my head was not shaped for it. For some crazy reason, black and blue Civil War hats (from the North) became popular back then. You could buy these hats at the neighborhood convenience stores. I used to love wearing my hats and colorful outfits, and therefore I have been open-minded and have admired the outrageous and unique styles that kids have favored over the years.

I took my dad school shopping once at one of these neighborhood shops, and he yelled at me and asked, "What the hell are we doing here?" in Spanish, of course. There were a mixture of potheads buying their paraphernalia; unsavory characters looking for tongue rings, nipple rings and all kinds of perverse imaginative rings; thugs in search of knives, martial arts weapons, and other types of weapons; metal heads hunting for the old black-and-white metal band shirts and posters of Black Sabbath, Def Leopard, or Metallica; and knuckleheads like me. How tough can you be when your daddy is buying your gear? I was doing well in school and to his credit he bought me what I wanted instead of storming out of there. He told me that next time he would just give me money and that he would never ever be caught dead in a place like that again! He added that he wouldn't tell my mom, and that was good because she would have worried. It seemed like I was causing my parents to keep a lot of secrets from each other, which seemed funny to me at the time.

We used to shop at low-budget, family-friendly convenience stores like Korvettes, Alexander's, D&D and Robbins. It seemed like everything was always on clearance. Most parents thought that getting great deals on clothes was more important than wearing new styles or anything fashionable. Unfortunately, many kids back then had to make the best of those hideous clothes picked out by their immigrant parents. Many Latino kids wore cheap, ugly clothing, but the trick was accessorizing and trying to devise creative, interesting looks. I used to cut off the sleeves off many of my shirts and do a lot of pushups to build up my arms to distract from the ugly shirt that I was wearing. The girls would wear a lot of bracelets and create unique looks with cheap clothes, kind of like Madonna in her early days. Even though we made fun of kids at school, we actually all understood and sympathized.

As we got older, we became embarrassed to be seen with our immigrant parents, who wore cheap polyester outfits, dress socks and shoes with shorts in the summertime, and no brand jeans or bootleg knockoffs. Our heritage was so rich in culture, so what happened to our parents? Did the great Latino civilizations forget how to color-coordinate over the centuries? The Ossa family used to go shopping at what looked like someone's house in Corona, Queens. It was always crowded, and no one spoke any English. You had to knock on the door and wait for someone to open and you had to give them a secret password or tell them that you knew "So and So" before they would let you in. There were always bodyguard types around the inventory. During the day they protected the knock-off inventory and at night they literally knocked people off. They were stoned cold killers, and these places were affiliated with the Cali Cartel. I would see bulges and pistol handles on some of these scary-looking dudes. I don't remember anyone even attempting to steal anything. I had an IZOD shirt that I bought from that illegitimate establishment. I wore it with pride, since only preppy kids and rich kids wore IZOD gear back then. I thought I was truly fashionable, until one day at school someone asked me why the crocodile (Izod insignia) was so small and sewn so high up on the shirt. I told him it was a new style that was not out in stores yet. There was some truth to that. This new style would never be in stores! There were also Polo shirts with a design that looked like a polo player riding a donkey instead of a horse. I stayed away from those shirts. There were designer jeans with misspelled brand names or missing letters. Sergio Valente jeans were popular then and I remember seeing just Sergio jeans with the Valente missing, or Gucci items that were spelled Cuchi. There were imitation Jordache jeans with strange-looking designs that did not resemble the originals. The trick was to wear long shirts to cover-up all the defects that were usually located on the back and front pockets.

My other cool junior high school friend was Omar. Omar was older than us because he was held back and was not promoted from the seventh grade to the eighth grade. Omar was a tough kid and considered a real "bad ass." Omar grew up in the hood just like I did but he did not have the family support that I had. His mother died when he was young, and he had a lot of family members that were bad influences in his life. He was tall, good-looking, quiet, and very charming until you got on his wrong side. A lot of girls loved Omar in the eighth grade and a few of them bought white T-shirts and had "I ♥ Omar" printed on the front. Omar was adjudicated as a juvenile delinquent and spent a year at a facility we called "Juvi". He didn't like to talk about it, but he told me once that he liked to work out a lot and read and keep to himself while he served his time. Our school was diverse, but I don't think anyone had ever met somebody who had done time in junior high school. As Omar's class had graduated when he came back to school, he didn't have a lot of friends. Mostly everyone feared him, as the rumors spread like wildfire. His classmates would make up outlandish stories like he had killed someone or robbed a bank. I know that if he had done any of those things, he would not be sentenced to only one year in a juvenile detention center. Omar didn't care; he thought it was funny and he enjoyed the fear and respect. I was used to hanging out with tough kids and we became instant friends; since Raf was my best friend at school, we all started hanging out together. The other kids were shocked to see us hanging out with Omar. The same fear and respect they had for him was transferred over to us. I remember one kid telling Raf and me that he would "kick our ass" because we were making fun of him, but then someone whispered in his ear, and he walked away. I found out that he was told that we were tight with Omar. I thought that was funny. I guess being good friends with Omar paid dividends since nobody ever messed with us. I used to wrestle with Omar and sometimes I would get the best of him. He was my friend, and I knew he would never try to hurt me. He talked about having martial arts and boxing training, and he described some of his street fights that were like mixed martial arts in the hood.

Many of us liked to wrestle for fun in the hallways between classes, after school or at lunchtime. In those days we loved the World Wrestling Federation (WWF), which became the WWE in 2002 after a legal battle over the rights to their initials by the World Wildlife Fund for Nature which was also using the WWF initialism. Vince McMahon, the owner of the WWF, was a pioneer and he put wrestling on the map. He invented pay per view and made them what they are today in all sports genres and all walks of life. I used to watch wrestling on Channel 9. Back then we had seven English channels and two Spanish channels and there were no remote controls; you had to turn the knobs on the TV to change a channel. Many old-school comedians joke about being human remote controls for their families. There was no cable, no MTV, no ESPN, no HBO, no Showtime; it was television's dark ages.

Many of us would watch wrestling on a weekly basis and come to school to show off our favorite wrestler's signature moves, although there weren't as many elaborate moves as today. We were all performing sleeper holds, full nelsons, fireman take downs, body slams, headlocks, arm bars, leg locks, bear hugs and your basic punches and kicks. Imagine a bunch of rowdy, overactive kids wrestling all over the school. The school was progressive, and they did not want to stunt our creative sides, but the wrestling was starting to get out of hand. One day in the hallway in between classes Omar accidentally bumped into a tall kid named Steve, who was over six feet tall, but he used to dress kind of preppy and was not known as a tough guy. I don't know what came over Steve that day. Maybe he was having a bad day, or he was angry about something. After Omar bumped into him, Steve flipped out, which shocked us all. Of course, Raf and I began to egg him on. "Oh, are you going to let him get away with that?" We were all just joking with him and being "smart asses." He should have just walked away.

Instead, he stepped up to Omar and started screaming at him: "I am sick of backing down, you are not so tough!" It was good that he was standing up for himself, but it was at the wrong time and with the wrong guy. When Steve lunged toward Omar, Omar reacted as nimbly as a cat: he easily side-swiped him, then quickly turned and jumped on top of Steve's back, wrapped his arms around his neck and put him into a sleeper hold. I had never seen anyone move so fast. As Omar applied pressure, Steve fell to his knees and continued to struggle until finally his motionless body went limp. Omar lay him down on the hallway floor gently. I had never seen anything like it.

By then there was a crowd around them; one of the teachers came running toward us and yelled, "What's going on here?" Poor Steve was lying on the ground unconscious. Some smart aleck said that he had narcolepsy and fell asleep. I thought about what they did during the wrestling shows on TV when a wrestler was unconscious, so I picked up Steve's head slightly and slapped him on the back of his neck. If you slapped the wrestler hard enough, they would come to, at least that's what happened on TV. Nobody understood what I was doing, and they thought I was just trying to hit this innocent kid while he was down. The teacher yelled at me, but suddenly Steve got up quickly on his own, started screaming and ran away down the hallway. To his credit, he never told on Omar. Nobody ever thought about messing with or standing up to Omar after that.

Carlito and Omar were not like Raf and me because they were not book-smart, but they were very street-smart and actually lived close to the school. Most of the students at IS 227 had to walk long distances or take buses to get to and from school, which was located in East Elmhurst near the famous New York prison, Rikers Island. The school was about a mile and a half west of what used to be Shea Stadium and is now Citi Field, the stadium where the New York Mets play. The USTA Center Arthur Ashe Stadium, where the US Open is played every year, is also near the school. As any fan could tell you, it is a scary neighborhood, especially after dark. My dad used to play soccer at the stadium where the US Open is played, and he used to take me when I was a kid. I actually saw the stadium being built and used to ride my bike all over the dirt hills and construction sites while the stadium was still under construction. When I was older, I even played tennis at those courts with my dad. Today only people with money can afford to play on those courts or watch the US Open Tournament. As a child, I took so much pride watching the US Open on TV, with John McEnroe battling Jimmy Connors, and Chrissy Evert challenging Martina Navratilova. I was not your typical New York City Latino kid because I secretly loved tennis. I felt connected to the sport because I saw the stadium being built from the ground up.

Today many of my former classmates from the Louis Armstrong School believe that the experience was one of the best times of their lives. It might be hard to find someone who would disagree, partly because before it was hip to be diverse, our school led the way with a mixture of Latino, Asian, white, Black, Indian, Jewish, West Indian, Irish, Italian and other groups. The school spirit and camaraderie was off the charts. Through social media, many of the former students still communicate almost forty years later. We even had a reunion party some years ago, which is unusual for junior high schools. I didn't remember everyone there, but I felt like I was with family. The organizers put together a nice event at a restaurant/hall near the school. There was a DJ and even some of the old teachers showed up. I took my wife with me, even though she thought it was pathetic to have a junior high school reunion. I didn't blame her for thinking that way since she did not go to our school, so how could she understand? It seems weird in today's fast-moving, impersonal, cutthroat world, but all the students were like family. I am not sure what type of research went into putting this new school/social experiment together, but unlike most New York City initiatives, this one actually worked! My sister works for the Board of Education as a social worker, and she told me that the Louis Armstrong School is still popular and highly regarded. I feel proud that I was there at the beginning of the experiment.

We had our graduation ceremony at a local college campus, Queens College. It was fun seeing all my friends and other students wearing suits. We were all making fun of each other. I was wearing an older cousin's suit, a hand-me-down. The school gave us caps and gowns for the graduation. I believe they tried to make it as formal as possible in order to lay the groundwork for kids to think about going to college. After all the speeches, everyone received their diploma and then the school band took the stage and played "Pomp and Circumstance." There were teachers, officials from the Board of Education, and even local politicians on the stage. There was a section in the front reserved for graduates and all the guests and family members were seated behind us. The ceremony was beautiful, and we were all proud to be graduates of the Louis Armstrong School. Everything went smoothly and we were all ready to leave to celebrate with our families when some knucklehead decided to fling his cap onto the stage like a frisbee. Of course, it started a chain reaction and everyone started flinging their caps at the stage. The officials on stage started ducking and scrambling for safety. The school band was performing in an orchestra pit that had been raised with hydraulic lifts, and it had to be lowered quickly. I can still see all the airborne caps cascading down on the band as the orchestra pit was being lowered. To this day, I still flinch during graduation ceremonies. When the ceremony was over all the parents started yelling at their kids. You could see moms hitting children upside their heads and dads chasing after their youngsters. My mother was angry when she saw that I was not wearing my cap. She yelled at me and told me to go get a cap for a picture. There were caps all over the place, but I still have a picture of myself with my friends Carlito and Raf and none of us are wearing a cap. There was no malice on our part; most of us were immigrant inner-city First-Generation kids, and we were just extremely excited to be heading to high school. I believe that the next year caps were banned from the graduation ceremony. Our apologies to the class of '84.

CHAPTER 7

The first time I visited Colombia I was six years old. My parents had worked hard and finally had a little money in their pockets, so they wanted to go back to their home country. I am sure that they missed their home country immensely; I couldn't even imagine how they must have felt. I truly didn't understand, until I took that first trip. I know that they cherished every moment, but I had some difficulties during the trip. At six years old, I took one for the team: I spent half the trip throwing up and getting sick. My stomach was delicate, and I was a city boy who was not used to the food or water found in a developing country with a tropical climate. There were no Poland Springs or Evian water bottles back then. After I got back to the US, I was mysteriously losing a great deal of weight and feeling weak. When I was diagnosed with parasites, I went to the department of health and was given some disgusting concoction to flush them out. I remember sitting on the toilet for what seemed like hours after I got home. My Tía Diana put on yellow rubber dishwashing gloves and basically shoved her hand up my butt. I could not check Web MD for a better solution because it did not exist, and I was only six years old, after all. Finally, after my Tía's heroic efforts I felt something come slithering out of my back side. It was a slimy, disgusting wormy creature. My Tía had a warped sense of humor, so she asked if I wanted to keep it as a souvenir! I don't remember my parents being there for that moment. Perhaps my Tía had lost a bet or drew the short straw. In all seriousness, my Tía Diana was a very sweet and loving woman. I cannot remember any important stages of my life when she was not there. She was a rock of our family.

Despite my health problems, my trip to the mother country in the early 70s was eye-opening, especially for a young city kid. My dad loved the ocean, and we did a lot of swimming and ate a lot of seafood. We went to Cartagena and Santa Marta, the fourth-largest urban city of the Caribbean region of Colombia. Founded on July 29, 1525, by the Spanish conqueror Rodrigo de Bastidas, it was the first Spanish settlement in Colombia, its oldest surviving city and the second oldest in South America. You could see the Spanish influence in all the distinctive historical buildings and prominent structures. The beaches, palm trees and lush greenery made the beachfront look like a beautiful painting. Just being there made me feel proud to be Colombian. It was all so captivating, and in my short inner-city life I had never seen anything like it. I saw a statue of the great Simón Bolívar, Latin America's counterpart to George Washington. My mom told me stories about him when I was a kid. Simón Bolívar was the greatest leader of Latin America's war for independence from Spain. He was known as a brilliant general and a charismatic politician who led the fight to drive the Spanish from the northern part of South America, called the Viceroyalty of New Granada. After the defeat of the Spanish, Bolívar contributed significantly to the formation of the republics that are now known as Colombia, Panama, Ecuador, and Venezuela. When I was growing up, I used to love history, especially anything having to do with my ethnicity and my roots. That evening, as I gazed at the statue in that majestic plaza, I contemplated Bolívar astride his horse and I could visualize the great battles waged against the Spanish soldiers, fighting to bring freedom to Colombians from the oppressive Spanish rule. It made me feel patriotic in a way that I had never felt before; I wanted to pick up a rifle and join in the fight. However, it was dinner time, so we had to go back to the hotel to eat dinner.

The next stop on our trip was the city of Cartagena, a major port that was founded in 1533 on the northern coast of Colombia, in the Caribbean region. It was strategically located between the Magdalena and Sinú rivers and became the main port for trade between Spain and its overseas empire, establishing its importance by the early 1540s. During the Colonial Era, it was a key harbor for the export of Peruvian silver to Spain and for the import of enslaved Africans. The slave trade was carried out under the Asiento System, whereby the slaves were brought to the Americas and a tax was paid to the Spanish crown for each slave that was imported. Unfortunately, this evil legacy was not limited to the United States. However, slaves were liberated much earlier in Latin America than in the US In Cartagena, I was pleased to see Black people speaking Spanish fluently. It makes me very proud to see people of different ethnicities speaking Spanish. There is a large Black population in most Latin American port cities, and all the people we met during our stay were very friendly and accommodating. Today, tourists flock to Cartagena due to the influence on the city of African culture, which is acknowledged and celebrated openly.

We had to take a boat to get to Cartagena. It was one of those old-fashioned ships, not a cruise ship, so I felt like an explorer with the wind at my back, looking out into the sea. As we approached the busy port, bustling with maritime traffic and activities, I noticed young boys swimming in the ocean near the ship. Most of these boys were Black and/or indigenous, and so thin that they were probably malnourished, but they were marvelous swimmers. The tourists would throw coins off the ship and the kids would dive for them. Apparently, that's how they made their money. Can you imagine swimming out in the middle of the ocean and diving for small coins? The shore was at least a couple of miles away. Perhaps you remember diving into a pool and looking for items on the bottom, while playing a game with your kids or siblings. Now imagine diving for coins in the middle of the ocean! Some of those kids picked them up quickly, while others took so long that it seemed like they were down deep in the water forever, but eventually they all would come up. It was amazing! I could not believe it. I am not sure where they would store the coins, but I am sure they had creative ways to keep their money.

    I was too young to remember everything about the trip, but I do remember that I finally met my grandfather, Antonio, for the first time. He was a tall, good-looking man, which makes sense because my mom was very pretty. Colombians are not known for being tall, but my grandfather was over six feet tall. I am told by my relatives that I remind them of him because of my sense of humor and joy for life, but unfortunately, I did not take after my grandfather in the height department. I never saw my mother happier than when she was with her dad. He was mestizo, which is a blend of indigenous and Spanish heritage. Back in the era called the Age of Exploration, the Spanish conquistadors did a great deal of exploring and had their way with many of the pretty indigenous girls. As a result, over fifty percent of Latin Americans are mestizo, including me. My grandfather was light-skinned with thick lustrous hair like a Colombian James Dean or Joe Jonas; even at his age he was youthful looking, which is a trait that many of us Latino mestizos share. We spent a lot of time together on that trip, and I remember that he made me laugh a lot.

On one of our excursions in Cartagena we saw a tightrope performer. He was a poor, Black man with ratty clothing, but when he stepped on that tightrope and started walking across a small river, he looked regal. I had never seen anyone do that in person. He walked from one side of the river to the other while holding a balancing stick. A large crowd of tourists had stopped to watch him. The tightrope was thin, and the rope must have been a quarter mile long. The river below was full of jagged rocks, and the distance from the rope to the river was like the distance from the roof of a New York City skyscraper to the ground. There were no safety nets, and I was scared for that poor man. During his long treacherous journey, I had my eyes closed half the time. On that day, instead of a bridge across the river there was a tightrope across the river. When he got to the far side, he turned around and started back toward the riverbank where all the tourists were gathered. When he finally arrived safely, he held out a basket and asked the spectators for donations after his death-defying performance, but he should have collected the money before he started. All those tourists and spectators, despite witnessing an incredible feat and giving a standing ovation, started walking away without putting any money in the basket. My grandfather started yelling and demanding that everyone contribute. My grandfather was an imposing figure and that basket filled up with money very quickly. My grandfather stuffed some bills from his own pocket into that man's hand, who then gave my grandfather a big, long hug. My grandfather looked like he wanted to cry. I was only six years old, but I will never forget that moment.

We continued our journey into the motherland and visited my Tía Celia's coffee farm in Sevilla, where my dad grew up. We had to travel deep into the mountains, and I got to ride in a

Jeep for the first time in my life. I saw all types of creatures that I had never seen before: instead of cockroaches, I saw iguanas; instead of subway pigeons, I saw colorful tropical birds; instead of stray alley cats, I saw beautiful jaguars; instead of plain, ugly and slimy city park worms, I saw colorful snakes; instead of creepy-crawly city rats, I saw agile monkeys swinging in the trees; instead of disgusting flies near the garbage cans in the summer, I saw beautiful butterflies; instead of disgusting New York City water bugs, I saw exotic multicolored frogs. You could clearly smell the fresh air and the lush greenery in the mountains. I had been struggling with asthma and allergies in New York, but even though we were at a high altitude, my breathing had never been better. It seemed that my lungs had mysteriously cleared up and my allergies had disappeared. When we arrived at the coffee farm, I wondered where we would be sleeping. All I could see were long fields full of coffee plants that stretched for what seemed like miles. Most of the coffee that originates from Colombia is grown on small family-run farms, most of them smaller than twelve acres. There are roughly half a million families working and producing coffee today. For many years, my Tía Celia was one of them. Sevilla is known as the coffee capital of Colombia.

    The land and the fields were beautiful, but the living quarters looked primitive. Just as I suspected, I ended up sleeping on a small, uncomfortable cot. We stayed there for about two weeks, and I learned very quickly that I would never want to be a coffee farmer. The farm hands would get up at ungodly hours to work the fields. Like in the movies or on TV, the roosters would crow early in the morning. Between the roosters, the uncomfortable cot and the buzzing insects that were flying or crawling everywhere, I barely got any sleep. The first time I had to use the bathroom, I found out that you had to walk to an outhouse, where there were no toilet bowls, just a deep hole above a wooden plank. There were always insects and spiders in the outhouse, so I peed in the fields a lot and held it in for number 2 until I was ready to explode.

The first time I had to bathe myself, I found out that at the farm everyone would bathe where the coffee beans were washed. So, what did that mean? Here's a little lesson, Coffee 101: Coffee beans (which are actually seeds) come from a fruit tree and the fruits are called coffee cherries because they are red when ripe. Coffee processed by the wet method is called wet-processed or washed coffee. The wet process involves removing the fruit covering the beans before they are dried. The coffee cherries are sorted by immersion in water: bad or unripe fruit will float, and the good, ripe fruit will sink. The skin of the cherry and some of the pulp is removed by a machine that presses the fruit through a screen, in water. The bean will still have a significant amount of the pulp clinging to it that needs to be removed. I remember seeing giant long sinks and vats. There was a small separate area in the coffee barn/wash house where the coffee beans were cleaned. The little wash area was used by the farm hands and had curtains and a makeshift tub. I felt like a giant coffee bean. My mother had to use buckets of cold water to bathe me as there was no running water. I felt embarrassed because my mother had not bathed me since I was a baby. The water was freezing, and the soap was brown, homemade and had a pungent smell. There were raw coffee beans in bins and containers everywhere and the smell was overpowering. I kept gagging repeatedly while I was being bathed.

There were many chickens and roosters on the farm. We ate a lot of fresh food, including fresh eggs for breakfast. The food tasted strange to me; I guess as a city boy you get used to all the preservatives and chemicals that they put in food in the United States. We ate fresh bacon and sausage made from pigs that were slaughtered on the farm. All this fresh food was making me sick and nauseous. Finally, the breaking point occurred when one of the farmhands asked me one day to pick a chicken that I liked. I was wondering why he would ask me that question; I naïvely thought that there was going to be some type of chicken beauty pageant. I looked around carefully and picked the biggest and most colorful one. The farmhand kept eye contact with me, smiled at me and then proceeded to grab it with his bare hands and snap its neck. I had never seen an animal die like that, and its sudden death made me sick to my stomach. I went for a walk in the fields because I was upset.

When I came back my dad told me to clean up because we were getting ready for dinner. Every night the family and all the farm hands would eat outside on a long wooden table. We were having sancocho de gallina for dinner. It is a hearty, traditional Colombian soup that includes vegetables, potatoes, yucca and the main ingredient, gallina. Gallina means hen in Spanish. I was starving because I was barely eating during the trip and my delicate city stomach was having trouble keeping down what little food I did eat. I started eating the sancocho and the farmhand told everyone that I did a good job in picking out the hen. I honestly believe he was trying to make me feel better but once I realized what I was eating, I became nauseous and threw up repeatedly. I could not eat anymore, and everyone was laughing at me and thought it was funny. As a result of my experience at my Tía's coffee farm that summer, to this day I don't like to drink coffee. I must be one of the few Colombians in the world that does not drink coffee. In an ironic twist, my wife and kids today love Colombian coffee. Most people around the world consider Colombian coffee to be the best. Obviously, they never stayed at my Tía Celia's farm.

Seven years later, in the spring of 1983, my parents told me that I was going to Colombia with my grandmothers for the summer. I was going to visit the mother country again, where my life's story began. I was excited, especially since my parents were not going this time and I knew that I would be able to get away with murder. My dad gave me a hundred bucks and said, "Hijo, here is some money in case you want to buy things while you're on vacation." I thought to myself that it would not be enough, but I was wrong. At that time, the US economy was strong and the American dollar was still the most powerful currency in the world. We flew on Avianca, the airline that typically went to Colombia. If you have seen Narco movies, you might have noticed that drug mules and traffickers were flying back from Colombia to Miami or New York City on Avianca airlines. Contrary to popular belief, only a minuscule percentage of Colombians are involved in the drug trade. A good analogy would be the Italians and organized crime; both Italians and Colombians get a bad rap. Hollywood has had a lot to do with that, especially because of movies like *Blow* with Johnny Depp or Netflix series like *Narcos*. Everyone in the world knows who Pablo Escobar is today. However, for the most part, Colombians are just hard-working, fun-loving people.

The flight to Colombia was fun and exciting because I saw a lot of people that looked like me, all in one place. The stewardesses (now called flight attendants) were all pretty. At that age, my hormones were out of control, and I was tempted to ask one of them out on a date. I don't remember seeing any shady or scary Narco types on the plane. All I saw were abuelitas and families looking forward to spending the summer in Colombia and reuniting with their families. Back then there were not a lot of tourists going to Colombia. The stewardesses were friendly and accommodating. Everyone was speaking Spanish and the whole flight reminded me of a family get-together. If they would have allowed food and music, the abuelitas would have been cooking delicious empanadas, arroz con pollo and tamales. The adults would be drinking aguardiente (Colombian liqueur that translates as fire water) and everyone would be dancing salsa in the aisles. I know that sounds stereotypical, but that's how I grew up. As far as stereotypes go, it's a fun one to have. Colombians love to work hard and then play hard and have a lot of fun.

The flight from JFK Airport in New York to what then was called the Palmaseca International Airport in Cali, Colombia, took six hours. In English, *palma seca* means dry palm. After sitting on those worn-out airplane seats in Avianca's Coach class for six hours, my whole backside felt like a palma seca. The minute I got off the plane, I realized that I was in a tropical country. The air smelled so clean and different. Everyone was wearing white, and many people were wearing straw hats. I learned very quickly that it was not a fashion statement or choice, but a necessity due to the intense tropical heat and sun.

Latin American airports are much different from American airports. In a Latin American airport, it feels like there is a whole lot of chaos going on. There are different categories of chaos, such as the large groups of families and relatives screaming and crying upon seeing loved ones that they have not seen in years. There are poor local kids running around begging for money, while indigenous women and children are trying to sell handmade crafts. You see soldiers wearing uniforms and carrying rifles and machine guns. You also see scammers and con artists trying to sell unsuspecting tourists fake or overpriced tour tickets.

The most insidious plots in Latin American airports are perpetrated by random taxi drivers who take unsuspecting tourists for a ride to a location where armed bandits rob the passengers of all their belongings. I am not saying that this is common in Colombia, but it is just one of the dangers of traveling to Latin America. I knew someone who was taken to a remote location by a rogue taxi driver on a trip to a Latin American country. He was held up at gunpoint, and they took his cash, wallet and credit cards. He was tied and blindfolded and was told that if he didn't give up his PIN, he and his girlfriend, who was also tied up and blindfolded, would be shot. Once the money was withdrawn from a nearby ATM, they were set free. Banks have limits now on how much money can be taken out of an ATM at one time. This happened while the young American couple was on vacation in a Latin American country. I am not trying to put a damper on tourism, I am just exposing the ugly reality of Latin American countries. The trick is to get picked up by friends or relatives, find a trustworthy cab service, or take a shuttle sent by a hotel, rather than take random cabs as you would in a big city in the United States. Inside some Latin American airports, you can buy a ticket for a licensed taxi, so the fare is standardized, and you are safe from thieves.

I knew that on our family trip we were not going to be staying at a fancy hotel like the Waldorf Astoria or the Four Seasons, but at my Tía Irma's house. She lived in a suburb of Cali called Benjamín Herrera, with her husband Fidel, her sons Pablo and Reynaldo, and daughters Jennifer and Leslie. They were my cousins, since Irma was my mother's older sister. I already knew the drill: I would either be sleeping in a cot somewhere or with somebody else in their room, or even in the same bed. I wanted to get to know my cousins, but not so intimately that I would sleep in the same bed with them. They had an old-fashioned cot waiting for me in a room already occupied by Pablo and Reynaldo. The house was modest, and it was certainly not big enough for all of my relatives, let alone any guests. What I noticed was that many of the homes in the neighborhood were painted in pastel colors. Some of them were nice looking and others looked like glorified shacks. It was like a bootleg version of South Beach in Miami. There were concrete sidewalks, but the roads were not paved yet. As we drove in from the airport, I noticed the dust flying and since we were riding in an open Jeep, I had to cover my mouth. I didn't care; I thought it was kind of carefree and exciting. The biggest hardship during my stay was that the house did not have any air conditioning. There was also no hot water, so I had to take cold showers every day, but the air was always so intensely hot that I didn't mind. Another strange thing that I had trouble getting used to was that when you used the bathroom for a number two, you could not throw the toilet paper into the toilet bowl. What? So where was it supposed to go? You had to throw the used toilet paper into a waste basket. So, when you opened the basket you could see what color the last person's poop looked like on the used toilet paper. It was like when we were kids in the United States, and we were taught that if your clothing catches on fire you stop, drop and roll. In Latin America you wipe, open the basket, hold your breath, close your eyes, throw, and close the basket. Apparently, it had to do with the antiquated plumbing and drainage systems. This is one of Latin America's dirty little secrets that tourists and affluent Latinos don't usually experience or know about because they stay at expensive hotels or live in fancy homes.

The day after we arrived at my Tía Irma's house, we ate a big lunch that included carne asada (skirt steak or flank steak), rice, beans, salad and avocado. After a tough first night on my uncomfortable cot, with a lumpy pillow, no air conditioning and sweltering heat, things were looking up. If lunch was so plentiful, I couldn't wait to have dinner. All my cousins were older than me and had to work and go to school. I was on my summer vacation but apparently, they were not. My cousins were all overachievers, studying to become teachers, scientists, scholars and professionals. My youngest cousin Pablo was on the Junior National Water Polo team. My cousins Leslie and Jennifer are now scientists employed by the Colombian government; Reynaldo is a college professor and Pablo is a coach for the Colombian national water polo team. He has been to several Olympics as a coach. After that big lunch everyone just lay around watching TV, relaxing, listening to music and reading. How boring! I didn't know that everything shuts down in the early afternoon in Colombia. It was called siesta. People would come home from work, eat a big lunch, relax for a few hours, and then they would return to work. I didn't feel like lying around while I was on vacation, so I went outside and started making friends with the neighborhood kids. They all made fun of me because my Spanish was flat and basic, and I spoke without the Cali accent. I quickly realized that it was just playful teasing, and I made a lot of friends that afternoon. We ran around, talked smack, played soccer… it was great! Finally, I was having fun on my trip. I was hot, tired, and starving when I came back to the house. I couldn't wait for dinner, but I had no choice since it was late when we finally ate. When I sat down at the dinner table, I was given a small bowl of chicken soup. I devoured that bowl of soup, and I was even slurping because I was so hungry and thirsty. I could not wait for the main course! Unfortunately, it never came. The soup was it! I learned very quickly that in Colombia, lunch is the main meal of the day and dinner is treated like a snack. I wish somebody would have told me before I arrived.

I became good friends with all the neighborhood kids. I often wondered if my parents had met in Colombia, would I be one of those kids? Nobody had stylish clothes and most of them were poor, but they didn't know it or act like it. I became popular because with the money my dad had given me, I would buy soda pop and candy for all of us kids. One thing I noticed about Colombian soda is that it is delicious. It is super sweet with lots of sugar, and the Postobon sodas had several different flavors. Postobon Naranja, my favorite, put the American soda brands like Fanta Orange or Sunkist Orange to shame. You can actually find Postobon soda in the United States. For all my Latino brothers and sisters, you could fill in the blanks with your own national brands like Country Club, Jarritos, Materva, Goya and the list goes on and on. They all have one thing in common: they are all delicious and bad for you. I believe these brands should be on the diabetes blacklist. My favorite lollipops were called Bon Bon Bon. In Spanish, a *bon bon* is a lollipop, and the Bon Bon Bons were giant lollipops, like super-sweet Charms blow pops on steroids. My favorite DJ today in New York, Alex Sensation, gave props to Bon Bon Bons during one of his concerts: "Best lollipops ever!"

We were all pre-teens and teens, and we were naturally curious about experimenting and having adult fun. One night a bunch of us went to the liquor store and bought a bottle of aguardiente. At the liquor store, no questions were asked, my cash was my ID. We were celebrating the birthday of one of the neighborhood kids, "La Mafla." (To this day I still don't know what that nickname meant to them, but I've found various definitions on the internet, including handsome, omnipotent, beloved by all and, in contrast, ashamed.) Everyone had nicknames in the neighborhood, and they called me el Último Americano Virgen, the Last American Virgin, because there was a popular movie out that year with that name. We all partied hard that night and La Mafla got drunk and had to be carried home. The next day his mom thanked me for making him a man. So, getting her underage son so drunk that he had to be carried home made him a man? We all became men that summer thanks to the Último Americano Virgen, who was spending the money his dad had given him. Just like in my neighborhood in New York City, kids were growing up entirely too fast.

My cousin Joselito lived close by my Tía Irma's house in Benjamín Herrera. He was my age and was my great-uncle Jose's son. In Latin America, kids are not often called Junior or the second and the third. In the US there was an old classic TV show, *Gilligan's Island*, with a character called Thurston Howell the III, an elderly millionaire who wore fancy outfits with ascots, and smoked a pipe. He drank martinis and wore a monocle like the old wealthy man who is the mascot of the board game Monopoly. In Colombia, nobody in their right mind will name their son Jose Vélez the second or the third. My cousin was named Jose, but everybody called him Joselito to distinguish him from his father. Another example of this Latino custom is my sister-in-law, who is called Irmita because her grandmother's name was also Irma. My wife's cousin Karen has a daughter called Karensita. My friend Rafael Sardina comes from a long line of Rafaels. The name is handed down from generation to generation, but the kids go by their middle names. Thus, it becomes Rafi John, Rafi Charles and so on. I like that aspect of my culture. It just seems ridiculous to add numerals like the second and third to some of the colorful names that Latinos have. Can you imagine? Florentina the second or Eliberto the third – it just doesn't fit.

My great-uncle Jose's mother was my Abuelita Hortencia. She lived with me in the United States and basically raised me because everyone else in the household had to work. La Abuelita Hortencia was like a second mother to me. I loved that old woman more than anything in the world. She was my great-grandmother. My great-uncle Jose's sister was my Abuelita Aura. I know it's starting to get confusing with all these names. La Abuelita Hortencia outlived two husbands, who both, according to the rumor, used to beat her and abuse her and her kids. Both of her husbands died mysteriously. Jose was almost the same age as my mom, although he was technically my mom's uncle. My Tía Daly is only three years older than I am. Such age disparities are part of the Latino culture.

This is where it gets interesting: my Abuelita Aura worked as a *criada* (live-in maid) in a wealthy family's estate. The man of the house had his way with my Abuelita Aura; she was raped, but of course he had a different version of the story. My abuelita never talked about it much. During that period of time in Colombia, the authorities were in that wealthy man's pocket, and nobody would believe her. When she found out she was pregnant by him, she begged him for help, but he called her a whore, fired her and kicked her out of the house. In Latino telenovelas/soap operas, a common theme involves the humble, pretty, sweet maid with the heart of gold, who falls in love with the rich man of the house. In the telenovelas there is always an evil second wife or girlfriend involved who treats her step kids horribly. It has to be a second wife or girlfriend because the Latino viewing audience would frown upon a maid stealing away someone's first wife. By the end of the telenovela, the evil second wife is either killed off or kicked out of the house and the viewing audience is happy and cheers. Unfortunately, in my abuelita's story, there was no happy ending, and the man of the house was the evil one! Her mother, la Abuelita Hortencia, was having trouble as well because her second husband had died. She was struggling to raise little Jose and my Abuelita Aura was struggling to survive with her young daughter Irma and her newborn baby Diana. I give my Abuelita Aura all the credit in the world because she had that baby even though she was violated and disrespected. That baby would turn out to be my Tía Diana. I cannot imagine my life without my Tía Diana.

While struggling to survive and on the verge of becoming homeless, my Abuelita Aura was introduced by a family friend to a handsome young man, Antonio. He could see that she was an honest woman with a good heart. They became friends and Antonio let Aura and her two daughters stay with him at his house. When he found out that my Abuelita Hortencia was also struggling with her young son Jose, he took them in as well. My Abuelita Aura and Antonio eventually grew to care for each other and had a baby named María del Carmen Campo Bejarano Vélez, my mother. My Abuelo Antonio helped to raise two kids, my Tía Diana and Tío Jose, that were not his own. I have been told that he treated them like they were his own children. My mother always spoke about her papá with great reverence. My Abuelo Antonio and my Abuelita Aura were never married, but they were great friends and partners. They amicably split up when the kids finished school. My mom came to the United States and brought my abuelitas with her. When she met my father, Jesús

Antonio Ossa, I was conceived within the first year of their meeting. My dad agreed to live with my abuelitas, my Tía Yolanda and her young son, my cousin David, as part of a package deal.

Fast forward decades later after I married my wife Sandy, her family was struggling because the company where her dad had worked for over twenty years was moving out of state. He was a couple of years short of a pension, but he was given a lump sum buyout. He was an older man and had trouble finding a job. He was forced to use that retirement money to support my mother-in-law and young brother-in-law, Eddie, who was an unexpected baby they had later in life. My mother-in-law, Juany Lanza, thought that she could not have children anymore and stopped taking precautions. On Valentine's Day, my in-laws celebrated my father-in-law's birthday, and she gave him the best present of all, birthday sex and the miracle baby was conceived. I consider it miraculous because in those days, my mother-in-law was usually healthy and rarely went for check-ups or physicals. Old-school Latinos generally don't like going to doctors unless they have to, so she only went to the doctor because she thought she might be pregnant. She found out that she was three months pregnant, but she also discovered that she had a lump in her breast. A biopsy was performed, and she was diagnosed with a malignant tumor, so she had breast cancer. If it were not for the miracle baby, that cancer would have spread and could have killed her. The only problem was that if she were treated with radiation, it would kill the fetus. I give my in-laws a lot of credit because they immediately made the decision that she would undergo a mastectomy, and her breast was removed. The miracle baby, Eddie Santos Lanza, was born on November 1, 1985. By the way, my father-in-law is Eddie (Edielberto), my brother-in-law is Eddie Santos, and I am Edwin. Eddie, Eddie and Ed. It was destiny. My brother-in-law had a son, and his name is Eddie Benjamin, following the Latino tradition. I even tried to persuade my wife to name one of our daughters Edwina, but she didn't go for it.

Since my father-in-law could not find a job and the retirement money was running low, my wife suggested that we all find a place to live together. Sandy and I were recently married and living in my dad's basement. So, we teamed up with my in-laws and the miracle baby Eddie, who was now a teenager. When we found a place to rent near my dad's house, we all moved in together. I believe we are starting to see a pattern. I hear people complain about having to visit or spend time with their in-laws during the holidays. They should try living with them. At the time, I had wonderful memories of growing up with my abuelitas, and I wanted that for my future kids. We now have two beautiful daughters, Christina and Liliana Ossa (not Edwina), and just as I hoped, they are growing up with a great deal of love and care. Sandy and I are working parents, and just like my abuelitas spoiled me, now my in-laws are spoiling my children.

On that summer of '83 trip to Colombia; I finally met my Tío Jose. Unlike my mom, he stayed in Colombia since he had a good job with the government and even owned a convenience store. He married a traditional Colombian woman named Karen and had four children: Arturo, Joselito, Markand Jennifer. Arturo was a few years older than me and Mark was four years old and Jennifer was a toddler. Even though we were all living at my Tía Irma's house in Benjamín Herrera, I rarely saw my cousins because they were always busy working and going to school.

Therefore, I often stayed at my Tío Jose's house during my visit, and my cousin Joselito became like a brother to me. He was short and skinny, but he was a tough kid and very smart. We were the same age and he used to joke around a lot and make me laugh. I barely understood any of his jokes, so it was usually the delivery that made me laugh. He used to joke about coming to the United States with me. He claimed to be small enough to fit in my luggage and sneak into the country on our flight back to New York. He even told my abuelitas the same thing. He was both charismatic and good-looking, and I believe that if he had been born in the United States, he would have been successful. People from Latin America love their countries, but there is a great deal of corruption and a lack of opportunities. Latin Americans want to come to the United States to try to make a better life, not for handouts or welfare, but for opportunities. What makes me different from my cousins? I was fortunate enough that my parents made love in the United States, and I was born in this country.

  I stayed at my Tío Jose's house as much as I could. Joselito and I were like brothers. When I didn't sleep at my Tío Jose's house, Joselito would come to visit me at my Tía Irma's house. On a typical night in my Tía Irma's neighborhood, all the locals would be gathering together outdoors: abuelos and abuelas on their front porches, men drinking aguardiente and playing cards, young teens holding hands and courting, families and friends playing dominos. I was surprised at how many skinny dogs would be running around and getting fed snacks by all the neighbors. In Benjamín Herrera, and I suspect that it was the same in many other lower or middle-class neighborhoods in Colombia, it was not like in New York City where people live in a house or an apartment for years without knowing or caring who their neighbors are. Everyone in the neighborhood knew each other and they all had each other's backs. Of course, when everyone knows each other and they are all like family, there is a lot of *bochinche*, or gossip. I found out that my Tía Irma was having trouble with her marriage from the *bochinche* in the streets. It was none of my business, but I felt bad because she was a good, sweet woman. Out of all my tías, she looked the most like my Abuelita Aura, so much so that you might think they were sisters. I could also see how my Abuelita Aura loved her and missed her. Irna and her husband Fidel divorced shortly after I left that summer.

Latin American countries have their rainy seasons, but I visited at the perfect time. The weather was good and the night sky in Colombia was always so clear, beautiful and magnificent. Every night was like one big party, with people gathered on their front porches, playing guitars and ukuleles and singing. The streets did not have to be cleared because there was no traffic at that hour. If you ask any Colombian that has immigrated to the United States, they will tell you that other than family, neighborhood camaraderie is what they miss the most.

One night, Joselito and I were playing with the neighborhood boys in the street, and a notorious bully and his crew showed up and started bothering us. He was bigger than us and a few years older and he was grabbing kids and going through their pockets. I had heard about this bully, but I was hoping to never see him during my trip. Most of these neighborhood kids were smaller and somewhat intimidated, and I knew that no one was going to fight back or stand up to this bully. I felt that something had to be done, but I was scared. Before I could say or do anything, Joselito confronted him. He was staring at him, eyes to chest, as the bully was much taller than Joselito. My cousin demanded that he leave us alone, but of course the bully replied, "What are you going to do about it? You can't take me and my crew by yourself." There were about ten other kids with him, all scary and tough looking.

Joselito said, "No, just you and me, one on one." The bully started laughing and quickly agreed, so we all formed a circle around them.

Joselito was wearing a long sleeve white dress shirt and slowly rolled up his sleeves and started stretching and cracking his neck and his knuckles. The bully had a curious look on his face, and he probably was thinking to himself, "What is this little runt doing?"

Joselito put up his fists in a traditional boxer pose. He started jumping on his toes and throwing jabs at the bully with a quick rata tat tat rhythm. He threw a left jab and then a right cross; the bully's nose began to bleed, and he looked dazed and confused. Joselito was giving him a boxing lesson. I didn't know that Joselito knew how to box. Everyone was cheering as Joselito was beating the living daylights out of the bully. Of course, his crew closed in and attacked Joselito. I jumped in and started swinging. It was Joselito and me against the entire crew. All the other neighborhood kids were scared and just watched. It looked like one of those old-fashioned, western saloon or bar fights with bodies flying everywhere. Those punks and cowards could not manage a fair fight. We were holding our own but eventually they might have killed us. One of those kids had a wooden board and hit me upside my head with it. I did not see it coming but I sure felt it, and then I saw that it broke in half with splinters falling everywhere. I was dazed but I have to admit, it didn't hurt that much, I was just in shock. When that bully and those punks saw that I did not go down, they all ran away. I think they just freaked out when they saw that board split in half on my head. I have always had a big hard head and my family and friends still make fun of me for that.

That night it came in handy. Joselito and I were heroes, at least for that one night. My Abuelita Aura told me that years later the bully and his crew would become *sicarios* (assassins) and the bully would go on to become a killer for the Cali Cartel. Joselito suffered a violent death on the mean streets of Colombia at the young age of twenty five. I keep thinking about a Billy Joel song, the one that says, "only the good die young." Rest in peace, Joselito.

During my trip, I also started working out with two of my new neighborhood friends, Lemus, and Bam Bam. Everyone in the neighborhood had nicknames. I'm not sure how Lemus got his nickname, but he was in good shape, and he was jacked. Bam Bam was a character from the *Flintstones* (*Pica Piedras* in Spanish) and he was smaller but was also jacked. I was getting there as I was working out a lot back then. We were all the same age, and if I lived in Colombia, they would have been my best friends. I was going to start high school in the fall, and I wanted to get in shape so that I could join the football and track teams. In junior high, I won the district meet in the mile for my school and broke a long-standing district record; I ran a sub-five-minute mile at thirteen years old. There was no one there from my family to see it because everyone had to work. I don't think my parents understood how fast I was. Once you start getting into four and sub-five-minute miles, that is considered world-class.

We were getting in good shape: in the mornings, Lemus, Bam Bam, and I used to jog, and in the afternoon, we would lift makeshift weights made with jugs filled with rocks. Near the end of my stay, they started talking about going to a diving spot called

Las Pilas, a waterfall located near the headwaters of the Cali River, in the mountains of the Cauca Valley. The only way to reach the waterfall was to hike thirty miles into the mountains. Even most Colombians don't go there because it is an arduous hike. The story goes that if you don't dive properly, you can hit one of the many jagged rocks hidden under the water. People would dive from the rocks at the top of the 30-foot waterfall into the pool below, which was a dangerous but beautiful watering hole. Over a period of about a hundred years, almost half a million people, including tourists and Colombians, have drowned, or been killed instantly by the hidden rocks at Las Pilas. One hazard at Las Pilas was the strong current, combined with an undertow that sucks swimmers under the water. If you just float in the water, the undertow will drag you down. Nobody just casually swam there; they would dive and then have to quickly swim to safety. The watering hole was about fifty feet deep, and another scary part was that there were underwater caves where unsuspecting divers would get stuck and drown. It almost sounds like an urban legend, but no, it was all true. There were also stories about giant pythons being found in the river. My parents had no idea what I was doing, so this was part of what I call my "secret life." I had adventurous Colombian friends, my vacation was ending, and I had to start high school soon as a freshman in New York City with God knows what kind of hazing and bullying in store for me. In the immortal words of the famous media personality, wrestler and actor Stone Cold Steve Austin, "Oh, hell, yeah," I was going!

    We got up early and embarked on our adventure. The trip would include a thirty-mile hike in the sweltering heat through treacherous terrain, through the mountains and toward the Cali River. We had no backpacks with provisions, no food, no water, no hiking boots, no maps, no compass, no problem, just T-shirts, shorts, and sneakers. Lemus was our guide because one of his friends from school bragged about going to Las Pilas and Lemus thought he could figure out how to get there. That was good enough for Bam Bam and me, so we set off on our trek, which first required walking through several neighborhoods in the city of Cali. We learned very quickly that Lemus did not have any idea where he was going. We got lost and to make matters worse, it was blazing hot that day and we were already tired and thirsty before we even got to the treacherous part of the trip. We were three kids looking to test our mettle and as we wandered through the city, lost and walking in circles, people were going to work or going about their business that morning thinking that we were a bunch of idiots. Finally, we reached a neighborhood called Granada, where the *bochinche* (meaning everyone knew everyone's business) came in handy. Bam Bam asked, "Yo, Americano, doesn't your abuelito own a store around here?"

He knew better than I did, because I had no idea where I was, but I said, "Let's look for it." We started asking around in the streets and we found it. We didn't have Google back in 1983, but the bochinche worked just as well (maybe better).

We walked into the convenience/sporting goods store and my abuelito was behind the counter. When he first saw us, he looked worried, as if he thought we might cause trouble. I could not believe my eyes: he was my Abuelito Antonio! I had not seen him since I was six years old. I wanted to jump over the counter and give him a hug. He recognized me from the pictures my mom had sent over the years. "*Mijo, ¿qué haces aquí?*" (Son, what are you doing here?) He was shocked to see me because this visit was not planned. He looked a lot older than I remembered and he was suffering from diabetes. He had struggled with his health over the years, but he was tall and strong and still looked like my Abuelito Antonio who I remembered. He embraced me and my neighborhood friends and invited us into the house. The store was located in the front, and behind the counter was his house. I met his wife, Margarita. My abuelito helped to raise my Tío Jose and Tía Diana, and with my Abuelita Aura he fathered a child who would become my mother, María del Carmen Ossa. When the kids were grown, he and my abuelita separated amicably. They were always good friends and partners, but they were never married. Margarita was a young, pretty Colombian woman and he was a lot older than her. She fell in love with his big heart and charismatic personality, plus he was tall and good-looking even at his age. They made my friends and me feel at home in their house. I was introduced to my Tía Carmen, who was sweet and pretty, and only three years my senior. She was going to school and working. My mom used to talk about her often, and I could tell my abuelito loved her. Carmen reminded me of my mami, and she looked like her and her dad. My stupid friends were looking at my tía inappropriately. I felt like saying, "Stop checking out my tía!" She had two brothers, Ruben and Arturo, who were also young and were technically my uncles. They weren't home at the time because they didn't know we were coming. In Latin America, older men who already have children from previous relationships frequently marry younger women. There are also plenty of Latino men who run around cheating on their wives and having kids out of wedlock, creating half-brothers and sisters. My mother-in-law's father was a colonel in Honduras and had multiple affairs. To this day, she is not sure how many half-brothers or sisters she has, but she suspects it is more than twenty.

Margarita made us lunch and fresh squeezed lemonade. We

were all so thirsty that she made at least three pitchers for us. I told my abuelito about our adventurous plans and he was excited for us. He used to love to hike and go on fishing trips. Unfortunately, years later he was cut with fishing hooks on two separate fishing trips, which led to the loss of both of his legs due to complications from diabetes. My abuelito knew that our plan to dive at *el Charco de Las Pilas* was dangerous, but he did not try to talk us out of it. It was fortunate that he gave us directions to the falls because otherwise Lemus certainly would have gotten us lost and we would have died of dehydration in the mountains. My abuelito told me that we were always welcome at his house. My friends thought my abuelito was very *bacano* (cool). I was so proud, and I knew that I would get more street cred in the neighborhood during my vacation. Sadly, I never saw my abuelito again. I know that he ended up in a wheelchair after he lost his legs, and the diabetes ultimately took his life. My mother died at a young age, five years before my abuelito died. He must have been devastated because a parent never wants to outlive a child. I know that they are together in heaven, looking over all the family members who miss them dearly; there are so many that I cannot name them all individually. I love you and I miss you, Mami and Abuelito Antonio.

My abuelito told us that Las Pilas was on the other side of the *Cerro de las Tres Cruces* (Mount of the Three Crosses), a famous mountain that had three giant crosses at the summit. You had to hike up five miles just to get to the summit where the crosses were located. The story of the *Cerro de las Tres Cruces* began in Cartagena, Colombia, centuries earlier at a famous mountain that was the home of a demon from hell named Buziraco. The demon was worshipped by the indigenous people that lived in a nearby village. The word quickly spread about the demon from hell, and the Catholic Church sent Friar Alonso de la Cruz Paredes to drive out the demon from the mountain. Friar Alonso summoned a group of villagers and drove up the mountain where the demon lived, armed with three crosses. Friar Alonso and his small army of villagers knocked the demon off the mountain by using the crosses, faith and prayers. Buziraco was driven out but was furious and was now looking for a new home, which he found in Cali on top of the mountain in el Valle del Cauca. The demon's power grew strong and in 1837 the city of Cali was mysteriously hit with many deaths caused by multiple plagues, including smallpox, dengue (viral tropical disease), leprosy and famine. In 1837, Vicente and Juan de Cuesta, two Colombian friars from Popayan, the capital of the Valle del Cauca in Cali, were sent by the Catholic Church to drive Buziraco off the mountain. They planted three large bamboo crosses on top of the mountain, which were eventually replaced by the three giant iron and cement crosses that are there today. Missionaries, lay Catholics and other Christians, as well as tourists make the pilgrimage during religious holidays, and masses are held at the summit, with a beautiful view of Cali. I cannot believe I went up there with my new knucklehead friends. We said our prayers when we finally reached the summit and then headed toward Las Pilas. Fortunately, we did not run into Buziraco, the demon from hell, even though the heat was so intense that I think Buziraco must have been close by.

    The terrain on the other side of Las Tres Cruces started getting rough. There were just dirt trails, and many rocks, trees and hills. The only sign of human activity was an occasional small village with makeshift huts and shanty homes, with no electricity or running water. The closest sign of civilization was on the other side of the mountain, where we had started our trek.

I saw a lot of poor indigenous people during the hike wearing traditional, handmade cotton clothing: women wearing makeshift dresses, men wearing shirts that looked like glorified coffee sacks, ponchos, moccasins, and handmade sandals. I saw a lot of wildlife, including iguanas, flashy birds, colorful frogs, monkeys, and strange-looking rodents. It was all beautiful.

However, the one thing that freaked me out was seeing snakes. I had never been that close to a snake before that day, but after walking for hours and climbing a mountain, there was no way that I was going back before we reached our destination. I remember seeing yellow and brown snakes with spots, as well as a grayish-looking snake with diamond spots. I was later told that this was one of the most dangerous snakes in Colombia. When I was a kid, my mom used to tell me the story of la Pudridora, a snake in Cali that would bite unsuspecting *campesinos* (peasants) out in the mountains. The bite would cause the area or body part that was bitten to rot. (*Pudrir* means to rot, so a *pudridora* is something that makes you rot). That story scared the hell out of me and now I was face to face with the infamous pudridora snake. The grayish-looking snake with diamond spots was la Pudridora, a viper that accounts for most snake bites in Cali and is known by many names and nicknames, including the Bothrops Asper, Cuatro Narices, Mapana or Equis. Even though these dangerous snakes are "bad ass reptiles," I noticed that they were not interested in attacking us; they just slithered on by us. Snakes generally don't bite humans unless they are provoked, scared, or feel attacked. Usually, tourists or hikers' step on these snakes by accident and are bitten because the snake feels threatened. Suddenly, this city slicker was turned into a snake hunter!

We kept walking in the sweltering heat for what seemed like forever. At last, we heard the waterfall. The sound of water cascading down the mountain was like music to my ears. We finally found Las Pilas! We ran to the diving spot, which was a circular opening in the mountains with a small waterfall dropping down into the Cali River. The actual diving area was small, and if you dove the wrong way you would hit the jagged rocks on the sides. There were a few kids and adults there, from ten to thirty years old. It was a very small group, because this really was a hidden spot. No lifeguards, no warning signs, just a beautiful deathtrap. There were tall trees with long branches on the sides of the mountain. Some crazy daredevils would climb to the top of the trees so they could dive from even higher than the normal diving spot. Diving from those trees was extreme. The distance to the water from the regular diving spot was about thirty feet. We had traveled so far, there was no turning back, so we were diving! We all took off our shirts and sneakers and wore only our shorts as we dove into the water. I was a strong swimmer, but I was scared to death. When I hit the water, it was freezing! I immediately felt the strong current and the undertow sucking me down. I had to swim hard and fast and grab the nearest rock just to get out of the water safely. Once we all made it out of the water, we had to climb back up the thirty feet to the opening in the mountain where the diving spot was. It was an exhilarating experience. On one dive, I nicked my ankle on a rock. I realized that if I had been a few inches to the right, I could have hit my head, and I would not be going back home to the United States alive. I had visions of coming home in a coffin. That was the last time I ever dove at Las Pilas.

 We left after about an hour, and the walk back was brutal. We were beyond exhausted, and I even drank some water from a well that belonged to a sweet *campesina* (indigenous woman who lives in the country). I didn't care what parasites, worms or diseases I would get by drinking that water because I was ready to pass out. We all drank out of a bucket from that well, and we chugged that dirty water like we had been stranded in the desert for weeks without anything to drink. The sun had set, and the sky was dark by the time we got back to the neighborhood.

My Abuelita Aura asked me, "What were you doing all day?"

I said, "Oh nothing, just goofing around."

My parents never found out about our crazy adventure. I passed out on my uncomfortable cot at my Tía Irma's house and I slept for what felt like days.

After my exciting excursion in Cali, climbing up the mountain to see the historic Cerro de las Tres Cruces, avoiding the legendary evil demon from hell who haunted the mountain; hiking for miles in snake-infested rough terrain and then cliff diving from the infamous Las Pilas and into *el Río de Cali* (Cali River), I finally felt that I was a true Colombian adventurer. That summer I spent so much time with my new friends and family that I even started picking up the Cali accent. I always thought that I am American only because I was conceived in the United States. My parents had both been in the United States for less than a year when I was born. I am proud of my Colombian heritage. So, this new Colombian adventurer from Cali was ready to fight for and represent not only Colombia but all of Latin America, like one of my Latin American heroes since I was a kid, the great General Simón Bolívar. This general helped liberate Colombia and much of Latin America from Spanish rule, and what he represents to Colombians is equivalent to what George Washington represents to Americans.

Unfortunately, unlike the great Simón Bolívar, I was still a gringo, and my American stomach and immune system reminded me of that fact and brought me back down to earth. During my great Cali adventure, I drank water from a *campesina*'s water well because I had no choice. There was no Evian or Poland Springs available back then. I became very sick and spent the remaining week of my vacation at my Tío Jose's house. I felt comfortable there and my cousins Arturo, Joselito and even little Mark and Jennifer felt like my true family. They made me feel like they could be my brothers and sisters. That would be the only place I would think about going to recuperate, other than my home in the United States, of course. I had a high fever and could not keep any food down. I could barely move, and I stayed in bed with multiple covers because I also had the chills. My Tío Jose's wife Karen took care of me. I was throwing up so often that I was dry heaving. I looked like the young Linda Blair character in the famous movie "The Exorcist." All my cousins looked scared and Karen would yell at them and tell them to be positive and keep up my spirits. They all took turns trying to keep me entertained and distracted, but I could see the fear in their eyes. Half the time I wasn't sure if I was talking to my cousins or hallucinating. Karen kept putting cold towels on my forehead. She had to spoon-feed me soup because I could not hold the spoon steady; she also gave me filtered water, tea, toast, crackers, and ginger ale. I honestly felt like I was going to die. I never knew anyone as nurturing as Karen, except for my Abuelita Hortencia, Jose's mother. My Tío Jose told Karen that I needed a shot of aguardiente and that would cure me. Every now and then when Karen wasn't around or when she wasn't looking, my Tío Jose would give me a shot of the "fire water," and it was so strong that I could feel my chest burning. My Tío would smile and tell me, "See, that means it's working." He was right, it did make me feel better, but when the alcohol wore off, I felt worse. My Tío Jose had good intentions. If my parents had known how sick I was, they would have flown to Colombia immediately and taken me home.

Over the years, I have found that Latino men all over the world think that taking shots is a cure-all. My wife became seasick on a booze cruise in Mexico during our honeymoon. One of the tour guides on the boat gave her a complimentary shot of tequila and told her she would feel better.

"*Tome, señora, se va a mejorar con tequila.*" (Drink up and you will feel better with a shot of tequila.)

I thought about my Tío Jose, but I hoped that this time it would be different. She was given a shot of tequila and instead of looking pale and sickly from being seasick, after the shot she turned green. She looked as green as the Marvel superhero the Incredible Hulk. I still thought she looked beautiful, even in a green shade. She spent the second night of our honeymoon giving tribute to the porcelain gods. I spent the whole night holding her head by the toilet bowl in our hotel room and giving her water and paper towels while she vomited all night. Now that is true love! That Mexican tour guide had good intentions, just like my Tío Jose. Thank God for Karen, who was so motherly and nurturing that she nursed me back to health. Even though I was sick as a dog, that was one of my fondest memories of my trip to Colombia that summer.

Throughout my stay at my Tía Irma's house in Benjamín Herrera, I found out that the entire family believed in and followed socialism and communism. They all preached the teachings of Karl Marx, Vladimir Lenin, Joseph Stalin, Che Guevara, Mao Zedong, Salvador Allende, and Fidel Castro. I represented the American oppression that had crippled Latin America throughout history. I was just a thirteen-year-old kid, but I guess they were hardcore with their beliefs because they never warmed up to me. I always felt like a stranger and an outsider at their house, even though they were my first cousins. I preached about the virtues of democracy and capitalism, but I was overmatched. They constantly attacked me and rattled off all the names of the dictators that were supported by the evil US government. They expressed their outrage as they spoke about how Latin American countries like Cuba, Mexico, Chile, Colombia, and Nicaragua, among others, were exploited by the evil Unites States government and big corporations. They read me the riot act about how Panama was not a real country and that it was stolen away from Colombia in 1903 so the US could own the land where the Panama Canal would be built. The United States secured their rights to build the Panama Canal by supporting the revolutionaries who wanted to gain independence from Colombia.

 My grandmother worked as a cleaning woman in office buildings in New York City for over twenty years. She was part of a labor union, and when she retired with a pension, she returned to Colombia to live with her daughter Irma and her kids. This was years after I had visited, and by that time Irma was divorced. Her husband, Fidel, left his family for a younger woman and even though all my cousins were professionals and worked government jobs, they all still lived with my Tía Irma and struggled financially. My abuelita supported the family with her pension and social security money until the day she died. While she was supporting the household financially, no one thought that her American pension was oppressive.

CHAPTER 8

I barely remember the flight home from Colombia. I had lost a lot of weight and was probably dehydrated, and I passed out the minute my rump hit the Avianca Airlines coach seat. Like most planes coming to New York from Latin America, the ride home presumably was filled with a cacophony of loud talking, babies crying and drama throughout the plane. Latinos are famous for having crying babies during long flights, church services and graduation ceremonies. I was oblivious to all of it, since I was lost in the deepest sleep I had ever experienced in my young life. When the plane landed, I was finally home. After being gone for months, I was very happy to see my mom and dad. When they asked about my trip, I just told them that I had fun; I never told them about all the adventures I had in Colombia. They were surprised that I was speaking Spanish with a Cali accent, a colorful and unique way of speaking that contrasts with the Spanish I spoke in the US before the trip, which I would call bland and plain, with no detectable dialect or accent. I finally felt like a true Caleño.

As I was growing up, I sometimes felt like I was leading a secret life. My parents and I never really talked much, and I felt like I was mostly on my own. They stopped helping me with my homework when I was in the second grade, which was fine with me because I usually didn't need their help and I felt bad when they got frustrated while trying to help me. I liked to learn on my own, and I was already reading classic novels when I was eight years old. My parents were always working and came home at different hours. We never ate meals together at the table, so I always ate alone in my room. When I see movies or TV shows with families sitting together eating dinner every day, it seems unnatural to me, especially when they're talking about how everyone's day was. When I think about reruns of the famous sitcoms *Leave it to Beaver* and *The Brady Bunch*, it's hard to believe that people lived like that!

    The day after I arrived from Colombia my parents dropped a bomb on me: while I was away, they had bought a house in the suburbs, and we were moving. I was leaving the only neighborhood I had ever known. The next day I wanted to hang out with my friends and get my last licks of the neighborhood before I moved to suburbia. I had been gone all summer. When I approached my friend Mario's block, I could hear loud music coming from what we called a boom box back in the early 80s, a giant radio with a handle. The bigger the boom box, the better. I saw kids who were barely able to carry their boom boxes that were half their size. Owning a boom box was a badge of honor back then. The breakdance revolution had begun, and I was late to the party. One summer away and it seemed like the world had changed. Everyone was wearing windbreakers, hoodies, Adidas sweatsuits and Kangols. Maybe you remember the hat that was synonymous with famous rapper and actor LL Cool J, which was called a Kangol bucket hat. DJ Grandmaster Flash from the Furious Five was one of the early pioneers of hip-hop who made the Kangol a part of his signature style, as was the Sugar Hill Gang's Big Bank Hank, who wore a violet Kangol bucket hat in the music video for the "Rappers Delight."

    In those days, B-Boys and dance crews wore T-shirts and jeans that came in different colors – black, orange, red, blue, white – and groups of kids would be wearing matching outfits representing a dance crew. All my old friends, including Mario, belonged to a dance crew that breakdanced. My friends Greg and Pete were "poppin' and lockin'." My whole neighborhood had been transformed, and now everyone was a B-boy. "Planet Rock" by Afrika Bambaataa and the Soul Sonic Force was blasting on everybody's boom boxes. I saw dance battles on the streets, as well as rap battles. Homemade linoleum, terrazzo or cardboard flooring was placed on the concrete and an instant dance floor was created. I found out that my friends Bobby and Joe were now neighborhood gods because they knew how to DJ and would rap and spin at all the local parties. Some of the others, like Lefty, were now graffiti artists. My boy Serge was now DJ Serge. I saw him a few years later in the city, wearing all kinds of bling and driving a white BMW. He was parked by the famous Tower Records store in the village in New York City and hanging out with a posse (his followers) by his car. We spoke for a little while, but he was not interested in reminiscing. I knew him when he was just Serge. Everyone had a tag (a symbol used as a signature) and some of the graffiti artists would sneak into the train yards at night and tag up the trains. Graffiti art was evolving and becoming more mainstream, rather than strictly underground. Graffiti experts were being recognized as artists rather than thugs that desecrated buildings, trains, and private property. The summer of '83 saw the emergence of the hip-hop revolution.

The four elements of hip-hop were breakdancing, rapping/MCing, DJing, and graffiti/tagging. Sadly, I was not good at any of them. My rapping skills were truly pathetic because my brain was not wired that way. I loved to listen to music, but I had no idea how to DJ or how to cut and scratch. "Cuttin'" and "scratchin'" were not aspects of my game. The classic rap "Sucker MCs" by Run DMC came out that year. So much great revolutionary music was being released, but I felt like I didn't fit in. I was not an MC; I just felt like a sucker! I always was a good dancer, but I could not breakdance if my life depended on it. I could dance reggae, disco, salsa, or merengue and I knew how to move my hips. I never learned how to breakdance or pop and lock. Some of these kids were like gymnasts on the streets, doing windmills, flips, back flips and spinning on their heads or elbows. These moves were amazing, and even more spectacular was the poppin' and lockin' (forcing your body to pop outwards or contracting your body inwards). Some of the dancers looked like robots while they were dancing; it was like pantomime gone wild. (Today the Jabbawockeez dance crew pays tribute to the original poppin' and lockin' dance crews and are often in movies and on television, wearing white masks, white gloves and Kangols.) It was truly breathtaking to watch. Unfortunately, my poppin' and lockin' skills were even more pathetic than my breakdancing skills. As for graffiti, I could barely finish my art projects in grade school, so I could never be a graffiti artist. Some of the murals and street art on the trains and buildings all over the city were elaborate and beautiful. The hip-hop revolution opened many avenues for inner-city kids, but unfortunately, not for me.

It was now the end of the summer, and I was depressed and exhausted. My dad made us move in early September before Labor Day. To add to my misery, he refused to hire a moving company. He was always cheap, but I guess that's how he saved enough money to make a down payment for the house in the suburbs in the first place. I was young and strong, but I was still only thirteen years old. He recruited one of the parents from the Boy Scout troop that I had joined years ago. They were a good family and lived in another part of the old neighborhood in a modest house. They were not like my typical street friends. My friends Al and Rick were volunteered by their father to help move the Ossas from the hood to the suburbs. Talk about exploitation and cheap labor. Moving from an apartment to our new house was back-breaking work. My dad rented a huge yellow Ryder truck, even though I didn't believe that he knew how to drive a truck. The biggest vehicle I ever saw him drive was our family station wagon. Years later when I moved with my wife and her family, my wife tried to rent a truck and the Ryder representative refused because she was allegedly not qualified or experienced enough. My father-in-law stepped forward and told the rental representative that he knew how to drive trucks. He said, "I used to drive trucks in Honduras," with his Spanish accent. He never even had his own car in Honduras.

"Okay," the Ryder employee behind the counter said, "now you can rent the truck." That's all it took, just a little white lie. No commercial driver's license, no experience, no problem. We all got into the truck and left the Ryder parking lot. A few blocks later my father-in-law got out and my wife Sandy drove the truck for the rest of the day. I am sure that when my dad rented a truck, he told that same little white lie, except he said he drove trucks in Colombia, not Honduras. Seems like all the dads drove imaginary trucks in Latin America. Truth be told, my wife Sandy was the best driver.

The morning that we moved it was chilly and overcast. The weather reflected my mood. I was leaving my friends and the only neighborhood I had ever known. I was not happy, and, in all honesty, I felt like I had been hijacked and I went kicking and screaming. We took 88th street to Northern Boulevard, then Northern Boulevard to the Cross Island Expressway, toward

Long Island, driving right past the Louis Armstrong School, the junior high school from which I had just graduated. It felt like I was leaving my entire life behind! As we approached our exit on the highway, I noticed a marina along the road with boats overlooking a beautiful bay. There was a path and people were jogging, walking and riding bikes. I did not notice anyone of color: Black, Brown, Latino or anyone that looked like me. When we exited the highway, there were no apartment buildings in sight, just beautiful houses everywhere. I also noticed that there were hardly any people walking in the streets. There were no stoops, no kids playing, no bodegas... what kind of neighborhood was this? When we arrived at the house, I must admit, it did look nice. But I was angry at my father, and I would not give him the satisfaction of smiling or saying anything positive. I understand now that my parents sacrificed to make a better life for my sister Valeria and me. We moved into a one-family ranch house with a finished basement for my abuelitas, and bedrooms for everyone. We also had a big backyard, big for New York City, of course. The funny thing is that we only moved about ten miles from where we previously lived, but to me, it seemed like one hundred miles. In New York, you can go from what is considered a bad neighborhood to what is considered a good or affluent neighborhood in just a matter of a few city blocks. There is usually a boundary line, but that line always seems to be changing.

My new neighborhood, Bayside Queens, was on the border of Queens and Long Island. My parents chose wisely because they bought the house for $145,000 in 1983, and then sold it for nearly a million dollars twenty years later. New York property values have skyrocketed over the years. Homes located in what used to be considered bad areas or working-class areas in New York, like Green Point, Carrol Gardens, Williamsburg, and Bedford-Stuyvesant in Brooklyn; the East Village and Soho in New York City; or Long Island City in Queens, etc., which were bought for as little as $10-20,000 are now going for $1 million and up. Baby Boomers have gotten rich selling their homes. Suddenly all these immigrant parents and grandparents, who had modest salaries and lived paycheck to paycheck, now think they are tycoons and want to give everyone financial advice as if they had predicted that gentrification would occur.

It is worthwhile to consider all the struggles that immigrant parents went through in these historically bad neighborhoods over the years. Even though lowlifes whistled at and harassed their daughters on their way to school and coming home from work when they were older, even though their sons joined gangs or were addicted to drugs and some even went to prison, even though their homes were burglarized multiple times, even though they had to put metal bars on their windows to feel safe, even though they often were awakened by the sounds of gunshots, they kept believing that the neighborhood would change. Abuelito, Abuelita, Mami and Papi were clairvoyant, like Nostradamus they knew that affluent white people – yuppies, hipsters, millennials, actors, and professional athletes – would want to move into their neighborhoods. They just knew it. That's the only reason they bought the house in the hood and stayed in a less-than-desirable neighborhood for decades. They were truly playing the long game, or maybe it was just good luck. Unfortunately for those immigrants and minorities that were not able to buy homes, they can no longer live in these areas because they cannot afford the new astronomical rents. Where do these unlucky immigrants and minorities go to live?

I had been living in my new neighborhood for a few weeks and I was miserable. There were no kids my age anywhere to be seen. I spent a lot of time talking to my mother and she helped me get through those early tough times. I had tried to go to the old neighborhood a few times, but it was inconvenient. I had to wait at the bus stop a block from my house, take the Q12 bus that came by every twenty to thirty minutes or so, and ride all the way to the last stop, which took about thirty minutes. Then I had to take the 7 train to the 90th Street stop, which took another thirty minutes. I was commuting for over an hour just to hang out. I was not going to work to make money, and I could not read the *Wall Street Journal* and check on my portfolio to pass the time. I felt lonely. In those days there were no cell phones, no iPhones, no tablets, and no iPads; I could not afford a Walkman, so I sat on that long bus and train ride alone with my thoughts and by the time I got back to the old neighborhood I felt like I didn't belong. I quickly realized that I would not be able to afford those trips.

My dad could see that I was miserable. He did not want me returning to the old neighborhood, so I had to go behind his back. My friend Greg, who lived on my old block, invited me to his birthday party before we moved. We used to be good friends but when I got back from vacation everything was different. My dad told me that I could go to Greg's party, but I had to call him at a reasonable hour, and he would pick me up. I was so excited to rekindle my old friendships and reconnect with everyone. I wore my best outfit: my red Lee jeans, black neon T-shirt and shell-top Adidas with the thick laces. I even took extra time to style my hair. I arrived at Mario's building because I didn't want to go to the party alone, and I hoped that we could hang out like old times before the party started. By then Mario had a new crew. When I arrived at his block he was hanging out in front of his building with his new friends, many of whom looked older than me. He introduced me but nobody seemed particularly interested in getting to know me or even getting to know my name. I just got a bunch of head shrugs, meaning "yeah, what's up." Mario had been my best friend since the second grade, and he was ignoring me to impress his new older friends. I tagged along with them, but I felt invisible.

We walked to a nearby park by an elementary school and the crew started smoking weed. The school was closed because it was a Saturday, but the optics were awful for pedestrians who could see a bunch of teenagers smoking weed in a playground. In my previous visits to the old neighborhood, I had smoked weed to try to fit in, but I never loved it. They were passing around a joint and I grabbed it when it was my turn.

One of the crew told Mario, "Yo, your boy smokes – he looks young." (I always looked younger than my age.)

Mario replied, "He is not my boy, I just know him from the neighborhood."

That felt like a dagger to my heart. "Et tu, Mario?" I took the deepest drag that anybody could ever take to show them that I belonged. I heard one of the crew say, "Yo, little man, don't hit it so hard – we put dust in that." (They had laced the joint with angel dust.)

When I heard that, I got scared but I said, "Nah, don't worry, I'm cool." I even took a second hit. Someone commented, "Yo little man got heart." Some of these guys were adults. The hardest thing I ever tried was marijuana and only a few times. If my dad knew what I was doing, he would have killed me. At the time I had heard about angel dust, but I didn't know what it was. Phencyclidine or phenylcyclohexyl piperidine (PCP), also known as angel dust, is a drug used for its mind-altering effects. PCP may cause hallucinations, distorted perceptions of sounds and violent behavior. Adverse effects may include seizures, coma, addiction, and an increased risk of suicide. At the time I didn't realize that what I was doing could literally kill me. I had moved to the suburbs, but I did not want to give up my identity. It was not a real identity, just a recipe for disaster. Unfortunately, I had to find out the hard way!

We walked from the park toward Greg's apartment building to show up at his birthday party. On the way, one of the older guys from the crew bought a forty-ounce bottle of Old English Malt Liquor. I was already high as a kite. One of the guys from the crew gave me the bottle and said, "Drink some of this, little man, it will bring down your high." So, I washed down the marijuana and PCP high with some Old E or Old Gold, as it was called back then. Bodegas in minority neighborhoods would sell beer to kids of all ages. I took a big swig because I had never felt that high before and I wanted to believe that it would bring down my high, but it just made me feel even more high, if that's possible. I started hearing echoes and hallucinating. When we were about a block from Greg's house, another older guy from the crew stopped at a liquor store and bought a bottle of Jack Daniels for the party. Greg lived alone with his mom, and she was visiting family friends; she was allowing her son to have a party alone with his friends because she wanted to give him some space. I wonder if she knew what kind of people her son's friends were. Greg was turning fourteen, but there would be no decorations, clowns, or party favors at this party, not even a birthday cake.

When we got to the party there were a lot of people already there: "B-Boys" (guys who are into hip-hop), members of dance crews, gang members, thugs, and scantily clad girls. There were teenage couples making out on the couches and a bunch of kids smoking weed by the open windows. There were candles and incense sticks throughout the apartment to mask the smell of marijuana. Greg told everyone to blow the smoke out the windows. There were some New York City pigeons hanging out by the windows that were getting seriously high that night.

I tried to mingle but I barely knew any of Greg's new friends. Before that summer and over the years I used to invite Greg to family outings, and we used to spend a lot of time together at his place and my place. I wished him a happy birthday and gave him a card with money in it. He said thank you and then ignored me the rest of the night. I did manage to ask him if Mario's sister Hannah was invited and he told me, "Don't even bother, you have no chance." I was just sincerely asking about an old friend, and I was upset by the way he answered me. Ever since I met Mario at the age of eight, his little sister Hannah always had a crush on me. She was just a few months younger than me. We were really just friends, but we would fool around from time to time. We never dated and I didn't like her in that way, but I would say we were always good friends. Hannah arrived at the party fashionably late with her new boyfriend, Flex. Yes, he was a break dancer, and his name was really Flex. He was older and everyone at the party seemed to know him. Hannah had filled out and was becoming a woman; I had not seen her all summer. She looked good but even that night I never thought of her in that way, I was just happy to see a familiar face. Perhaps I was too excited or overzealous, but I went to say hi to her immediately and she just said, "Oh hi." She did not even utter my name. I had known her since I was eight years old, and we had been intimate friends, but she did not think enough of me to introduce me to her boyfriend Flex. At that moment even though there were nearly one hundred people stuffed into that smoked-filled fire hazard of a small apartment, I felt like I was alone. There was a liquor table that was stacked with bottles of rum, vodka, Jack Daniels, soda, plastic cups, and ice. I knew Greg's mom was a good Haitian woman, and she never would have allowed any of this. Everyone brought their own liquor, just like Mario's crew and I am sure that liquor table was set up after she left to see her friends. She would not have condoned what was going on. The worst part about that party was that I was not the youngest one there.

I wanted to call my father to pick me up, but I was scared because I was still high. I knew that he would punish me and hit me if he saw me looking that way. I wanted to give it a couple of hours and then hopefully it would wear off. I wanted to try to fit in, so I started drinking. I hit the liquor table hard. I started making myself Jack Daniels on the rocks, one after the other, to wipe away my high and my feelings of inadequacy. I heard one of the guys from Mario's crew say, "Yo, little man is drinking, he's hardcore." He knew what I was on. Finally, someone was paying attention to me. After an hour of drinking, all the voices at the party started sounding like they were slowing down and eventually everything, including the voices, morphed into slow motion. All I could hear were muffled sounds, then the room starting spinning and I started feeling dizzy. I felt scared and panicky. I wanted to lie down because I felt like I was ready to pass out, so I stumbled toward one of the couches. At that point,

I could hear laughter like in the scene from the Stephen King book that was made into the movie *Carrie*, at the prom after the bully teenagers dropped pig blood on her and everyone at the prom started laughing at her. She then uses her telekinesis powers to kill all the bad kids and destroy the school. Sadly, I had no such powers, so I just fell on the couch next to some stupid teenagers that were making out and doing some heavy petting.

At that very moment, a calm and peaceful feeling came over me. I didn't hear anyone laughing anymore or making fun of me. I started seeing my young life in a movie, starting from the first scene when I was a baby, like a dream. As an adolescent, how could I remember being a baby and then a toddler? Teenagers are not supposed to have memories of when they were babies or toddlers. I could see those moments vividly, observing the younger me with my abuelitas, my papá, my mami, my Tía Diana. There is a saying that when you are dying, just before you die your life flashes before your eyes. It really was like watching a movie and my young life was flashing before my eyes. Watching that movie made me feel so good and gave me a warm, peaceful feeling. I was so happy because it had been such an awful night. Once the movie reached the present on that fateful night, it ended abruptly but then something even better happened: a feeling of euphoria came over me, and I felt both ecstatic and peaceful. I saw a bright, round tunnel open up and I was traveling through it. I did not see my body, but I just felt like I was flying through it. There were bright lights throughout the tunnel, but as I traveled through it, I saw an even brighter light at the end. It is hard to describe that light at the end of the tunnel with words. It was the brightest, most radiant light I had ever seen. The tunnel itself was the color of neon lights, but that light at the end was as bright and dazzling as anything I had ever seen. The only thing I could compare it to was traveling into the sun itself. I felt so carefree, and I did not want to stop before I reached that bright light. Then suddenly everything came to a screeching halt! I just opened my eyes and saw adults and kids standing over my lifeless body and it looked and felt like I was on a cold bathroom floor. I heard the muffled voices again. The next time I woke up I was in my bed in my house, and I felt bruises everywhere and my entire body was sore.

I immediately went into my parents' bedroom and asked, "What happened?" Obviously, I knew what happened, but I wanted to know how I got into my own bed. My dad starting yelling: "Wha happin', wha happin'?" just like that, with his Spanish accent.
 He rushed toward me like he wanted to kill me, and my mother screamed, "No, Tony, no! Edwinsito has had enough!" My dad stopped himself and told me to go back to my room. Later that day my mom came into my room. I immediately started crying and told her, "I'm sorry, Mami, I am so sorry." I was embarrassed and ashamed. My mom was never judgmental; she just calmed me down and told me that she loved me. She then explained what happened in detail.

Someone from the party, probably Greg or Mario, called my house and said that I was sick and had to be picked up. That was the first mistake. If there had been responsible adult supervision – and I say responsible because some of those boneheads at the party were technically adults – an ambulance would have been called. My mom and dad came to pick me up in the family car, a long, maroon-colored Chevrolet station wagon with a lot of space in the back. When my parents arrived, I was lying on the bathroom floor. Greg's mother had been called by then. She told my parents that I was a troubled kid and that I needed help. My dad was beyond furious. He scraped me off the ground, carried me out like a sack of potatoes, and dumped me into the back of the station wagon like a corpse in a hearse. That was the second mistake. I should have been taken to the hospital immediately. My mom told me that she wanted to cry because when she saw my lifeless body on the bathroom floor, it looked like my eyes had rolled back and she could see the whites of my eyes. My dad did not take me to the hospital; he just drove us home, took my lifeless body out of the station wagon and dragged me into the house. He carried me a short distance and then threw me to the ground in the kitchen, like a bag full of trash. As I lay motionless on the kitchen floor, he began to punch and kick me repeatedly. That was another mistake. That explains all my bruises and body soreness. My mom, Abuelita Aura and Abuelita Hortencia were screaming at him to stop. Finally, my abuelitas threw themselves on top of me, acting as human shields. My father stopped hitting me because he would have hit my abuelitas if he continued. He stormed away into his room. It seemed like my dad was more intent on beating me to a pulp than helping his poor son, who had obviously made a terrible mistake. My grave blunder was due to wanting to fit in, and feelings of helplessness and insecurity, rather than any defiant rebelliousness. To this day, I still do not believe that my father ever understood. My abuelitas and my mom changed my clothes and put me in bed. My mother was always honest with me, and we could talk about anything and everything; she was my best friend. I never spoke to my father about that night again.

I never went back to my former neighborhood to see my old

friends. My dad didn't have to tell me; I just knew that I could never recapture my youth and it was time to move on with my life. The year before we moved to the suburbs, my best friend in junior high school, Raf, told me that he was taking an exam to get into one of New York City's specialized high schools. At that time there were three specialized high schools: Stuyvesant High School in New York City, Bronx High School of Science, and Brooklyn Technical High School. Every year 30,000 junior high school students take the specialized high school exam and only a few thousand are accepted. The career or area of study you wanted to pursue would determine your top choice. Kids could be accepted to all three and then have to make a difficult decision. Thus, twelve- and thirteen-year-olds had to know what career would be best for them. Talk about pressure. Did I want to become a psychologist, rocket scientist, mathematician, chemist, biochemist, physicist, engineer, architect, doctor, lawyer, writer, CEO, entrepreneur, or college professor? I thought, "So many choices! How about 'undecided,' since I am only a kid?" It would be an understatement to say that it was super competitive to get into one of these schools. By attending one of these specialized schools for free, I would get an education equivalent to the training at an expensive private school or an elite boarding school. Only the best of the best were accepted, but it was based on test scores, not what neighborhood you were from, what your last name was, who your parents knew or who your relatives were. As a point of reference, Stuyvesant was considered to be like Harvard University, Bronx Science was like Yale and Brooklyn Tech was like Princeton University. They were all elite and all specialized in different areas.

Once Raf told me about the specialized tests, I made some

inquiries at my junior high school and was able to get an application from one of my teachers. The test was called the Specialized High Schools Admissions Test, the SHSAT. One day after school I was hanging out with my friend Greg in the old neighborhood before I moved to the suburbs, and I told him I was going to take the SHSAT and try to get into one of the specialized high schools. His reaction was: "Why the hell are you going to take the SHIT test to get into some stupid school that doesn't want you, when you could go to Newtown like everyone else in the neighborhood?" Newtown was the designated high school for kids in our neighborhood. Almost everyone I knew went to Newtown, including Greg, Mario and Hannah. I took the "SHIT test" and was accepted to Brooklyn Technical High School.

My first childhood friend, Mario, became addicted to crack cocaine and struggled with his sobriety for years, spending time in various rehab facilities. My good pre-teen friend, Greg, was convicted for drug dealing and cocaine possession and served time in prison. I didn't feel any type of satisfaction – even though at his birthday party his mother told my parents that I was troubled, and I almost died because the neighborhood victimized so many of us kids – on the contrary, I felt empathy. My junior high school buddy, Omar, also would serve time in prison for drug dealing and cocaine possession. I heard that my friend Robby, known as Dracula in the neighborhood, was shot to death as a teenager. JoJo was arrested for armed robbery and did some hard time. Frank Melendez, my old Boy Scout friend, joined a notorious gang in Corona Queens. He was involved in a robbery gone bad; ironically, the robbery occurred at a social club near where we used to have our Boy Scout meetings. There was a hostage situation and Frank Melendez and the hostage were gunned down by the police. There was some controversy because the police tried to pin the death of the hostage on Frank and his crew, even though forensics showed that the police actually killed the hostage. Frank was shot over forty times. No officer was ever charged with any crimes and no investigation was ever ordered. Frank Melendez was only sixteen years old. One of my other good Boy Scout friends, Joey, was charged with armed robbery and murder for the same failed heist. My other Boy Scout friend Johnny, who was part of the same gang, was also convicted and did hard time for another armed robbery. I had been in all their homes and knew their families. Before Frank's demise, I had never been to a funeral for someone my own age.

When we were kids, Frank always struggled with the idea of getting respect in the streets. The neighborhood code was that you were either soft or hard; if you wanted respect, you had to earn it. I recall once that we were in a playground near his home in Corona, in a tough neighborhood. We were playing basketball and some thugs told us to leave because they wanted the court. We were just kids, and they were older, but they didn't care. When Frank didn't want to leave, they threatened to take our gear and sneakers. We were told, "If you lil motherfuckers don't get the fuck out of here we are going to run your shit (take your stuff)." Frank wanted to fight but I talked him out of it and convinced him to leave with me. He told me that one day he would be feared and respected. He joined a gang and was feared and respected by thugs that knew nothing about what true respect was. I did not see any thugs at his funeral, just his friends and family that always loved him unconditionally. Where did fear, respect, street cred and money get him? When I saw his poor parents and sister crying hysterically and inconsolably in that funeral parlor, I wished that he could have seen that he had all the respect that he needed from the people that truly loved him and cared for him. That was the first time I ever cried in public. Rest in Peace my old friend, you left us too soon. I only have mentioned my close friends. I can't even imagine what happened to some of the other kids I knew over the years in the old neighborhood. I am sure there are many First-Generation Latinos who have their own heart-wrenching stories to tell.

I went back years later with my girlfriend, Sandy (now my wife), to visit my Tía Diana. My tía still lived in the same building where I grew up, but she was moving to a condo in a better neighborhood. Some scraggly guy was lying on the ground near the elevator, and he was obviously strung out. He looked up at me and said, "Yo, I know you."

Sandy, in utter disbelief, exclaimed, "Edwin, who the hell is that guy?"

I honestly had no clue.

Then he blurted out, "You used to hang out with Jojo, Dracula and the crew."

"Yes, you're right, I used to hang out with Jojo and Dracula, but that was a long time ago. A long time ago," I repeated to myself, trying to create some distance. But then I looked carefully at that poor kid and the memories came rushing back to me. Perhaps if things had been different, I would have been the one sprawled on the ground.

CHAPTER 9

My first day at Brooklyn Tech High School was more difficult than most. The commute from my new house in Bayside, Queens, was a killer: I had to leave at least two hours early to make sure that I would not be late. I woke up at five thirty a.m. and left the house by six thirty when it was still dark outside. First, I had to walk one block to the bus stop and wait for the Q12. Usually at that hour in the old neighborhood, there would be people still milling around after a night of doing God knows what. That morning, however, I was alone on the street. I had to ride the Q12 bus to the last stop in Queens, which took thirty to forty five minutes, depending on traffic. Then I had to take the 7 train to the 74th Street Roosevelt Avenue station, which took another half hour or so.

Some years later, a white major league baseball pitcher for the Atlanta Braves, John Rocker, who was born and raised in Statesboro, Georgia, made disparaging remarks during an interview about riding the 7 train. The 7 train stops at the home of the New York Mets, then Shea Stadium and now Citi Field. He compared it to the war-torn Middle East and labeled the commuters as losers and degenerates, specifically including young single mothers. He made multiple homophobic slurs and disparaged immigrants, and First-Generation Latinos just like me. I only saw hard-working immigrants and First-Generation men, women, teenagers, and kids trying to survive and taking the

7 train to get to school or work. As much as I don't want to believe it, there may be segments of the population in the United States that may still feel the same way as John Rocker did, over twenty years later!

After taking the 7 train, I had to transfer to the E Train and take that to Queens Plaza, which took another ten minutes. I felt out of place taking trains and buses with grown men and women who were commuting to work in the morning. Everyone looked miserable and they all were in a hurry. The 7-train traveled from Flushing Queens to 42nd Street and Times Square in New York City. The platform was jam-packed, and everyone rushed to their seats as if they were competing in a giant game of musical chairs. It was analogous to the beginning of a horse race when the announcer hollers "They're off!" and the investment banker takes the lead, but the nurse is right on his heels! Every commuter was always in a big rush to get a seat. It was survival of the fittest, which reminded me of Charles Darwin's theory, as well as *Lord of the Flies*, a book I read in elementary school. I certainly was not the Lord of the Subway. I was too slow that first morning and someone sat in my spot as I tried to sit, but I squeezed in right next to him, and then someone almost sat on my lap as they tried to grab the seat. Another strange phenomenon that occurred with great frequency was that these commuters, who were super aggressive and ready to kill for a seat, once they sat down, would shut their eyes, and go to sleep. Sometimes it was not just a nap, but rather deep sleep, including snoring and drooling. Over the years I have had more than one person nod off and put their head on my shoulder. You could be polite and shrug your shoulder or nudge their head. If that tactic did not work, you had to wake them up and then they would be offended that you woke them up and refused to serve as a human pillow.

Another fun part about riding on the subway in New York City occurs when homeless people decide to use subway cars as hotel rooms. Instead of luggage, they use shopping carts or garbage bags full of old dirty clothes, and who knows what else. The stench is overwhelming. The homeless also sometimes use the subway seats as beds. Over the years I have seen many homeless individuals lie on a subway seat as if they were in a nice comfortable bed at the Waldorf Astoria, or for those of us that are more familiar with more modest hotels, a Holiday Inn. Over the years commuters in New York City have been so hardcore and desensitized that they brave the smell and sit near or even next to the "sleeping beauty" homeless individual.

Back to my first day of school commute, then at Queens Plaza I had to transfer to the G train to Fulton Street in Brooklyn, which would take another half hour. While waiting for the G train to arrive, I saw one of my friends from the old neighborhood: a disgusting New York City rat walking on by and just "chillin'" on the train tracks! The rat was so big it looked like a fat cat! I hadn't had to deal with or see rats close up after my family moved to the suburbs. The rat looked much more at ease and comfortable than me because I was always freaking out whenever I saw a cockroach or a rodent after growing up in the hood. I suppose that I was traumatized, but back then who could afford therapy for traumatic experiences with New York City creatures? The timetable that I just described does not take into account any delays, and there were always delays due to a multitude of reasons. Over the years, you hear them all. The most popular one is that trains are delayed due to congestion ahead. Trains also are delayed due to a criminal investigation when someone is robbed or killed at a nearby subway stop. Sometimes there are reports of suspects fleeing on the train tracks from station to station. Trains are delayed when a passenger becomes sick and is awaiting medical attention for heart attacks, strokes, epileptic seizures, and all kinds of medical conditions. If any of these medical emergencies involved a relative or a loved one, any commuter would be concerned, but because it is not a relative or a loved one and these potential life-threatening conditions are delaying the commute, most people are thinking, "Get them the hell off the train and take them anywhere else but here!" Unfortunately, becoming desensitized to these types of sad and horrendous things is part of becoming a typical New Yorker.

In the summer the underground stations and platforms get hot due to poor ventilation and a lack of air conditioning. The temperatures can go up to over 120 degrees in extreme cases. In the winter the subway rails sometimes crack in the cold weather, the antiquated signals malfunction and trains even derail from time to time. The New York City subway has the worst OTP (on-time performance) of any major transit system in the world. There is an emergency cord on each subway car and if the cord is pulled the train will immediately come to a stop. Sometimes passengers fearful of being mugged or assaulted would pull the cord, or knuckleheads would pull the cord just for kicks. The New York City subway system was considered dangerous back in the late 70s to mid-80s. If you relied on the subway to get anywhere in those days, you had to cross your fingers and pray for the best. (This is still the case, but perhaps to a lesser extent.) With a birthday coming up in November, I was still thirteen years old on my first day of commuting to high school. It was surreal and hard to comprehend that I would be making this commute every day, round trip, for the next four years. Yikes!

When I finally arrived after my long subway journey, I walked toward my new school in amazement. The building was enormous and looked like a castle to me; the only thing missing was a moat. I saw a huge radio antenna on the roof and was surprised to learn that the school had its own radio station! In any given year, the enrollment would be about five thousand students, from all types of ethnic backgrounds and neighborhoods. There are five sections to the building: north, south, east, west and center, which connects east to west. There are nine floors as well as a basement where classes are held. There were so many kids that I felt like I was at a college campus, but in spite of the diversity, I did not see a lot of people that looked like me. Even though there were not a lot of Latinos, it didn't matter because over the years I felt that everyone was treated with respect. We all knew how hard it was to get into the school, so all the students were considered to be among the "best of the best." Nobody thought about racial barriers. I am sure that the racial breakdown and percentages over the years may vary, but during my time at the school, there were students who identified as: Black, Jamaican, West Indian, African, white, Italian, Irish, Jewish, Asian, Chinese, Japanese, Korean, Latino, Puerto Rican, Mexican, South American, Central American, Dominican, Indian, Arabic, Greek and Middle Eastern. Smart kids in New York City come in all sizes, shapes and colors. I am sure that many parents bristled with pride when their sons or daughters were accepted to Brooklyn Tech: First-Generation families, families who struggled with poverty, families that escaped from political turmoil in other countries, families who suffered due to a lack of opportunities, legacy parents who had an alumnus graduate in the family, and established families that also were proud of their kids. There may have been celebratory parties in some of the households, or a simple expression of joy in other households. There may have been unwanted pressure on young teenagers to excel and work harder than everyone else to achieve their dreams. At the end of the day, we were all just kids, hoping for a chance to breathe and enjoy the moment.

Nevertheless, being a freshman in high school was like going to prison for the first time. I know that sounds extreme, but that's the only comparison I can make. Not that I have any personal experience, but today we all have seen enough prison movies, TV shows, and cable series like Netflix's *Orange Is the New Black* to know what prison is like. In high school, instead of an orange jump suit, you wear clothing that is not quite up to snuff. As freshmen, most of us still couldn't get a job and had to rely on our parents to buy us clothes, and you know how that goes! If we were lucky, they would just give us the money and not try to surprise us with clothes they picked out for us.

"Seriously, Ma, spandex pants with zebra stripes?" or "Really, Dad, a green flowered shirt?"

Our parents would say things like "Stop complaining. I asked the salesperson at JC Penny, and he said it was in style." Sure, they were looking for a sucker to unload clothes that no one would buy! In those cases, you might as well wear a sign on your forehead that said, "Please pick on me"! Lee colored jeans had been popular back in the early 80s, but when I started high school, the old-fashioned multicolor Lees were out of style. I didn't get the memo, and I had so many different colored pairs. Maybe I could have my abuelita sew them all together and make a giant multicolored blanket that I could hide under. How could they go out of style so fast? I was hoping to rock my collection for one more year. I struggled with my wardrobe that first year, among other things.

Going to lunch in the cafeteria was terrifying the first few days. Where do I sit? I can honestly say that I did not know anyone when I started my freshman year at Brooklyn Tech. Everyone was looking to make alliances. I met a student that had the same name as me, Ed and he was part Latino, which was good enough for me. Wow, I thought, we had so much in common! Actually, we had absolutely nothing in common, but we helped each other early on, and we did not have to sit alone at lunchtime. He loved art and rock music, and I loved sports and hip-hop, but more importantly, we loved not having to sit alone. We sat together for a few weeks until we met other people who shared our interests.

I joined the track and football teams as soon as possible. The best way to stay protected as a freshman was to join a sports team, like joining a gang in prison. I loved both track and football, and I was super-fast. I didn't let the fact that I was five-foot-five and weighed about 150 pounds stop me. I did not play football early in my freshman year because the season started in the fall. All the practices and football camp for most incoming freshmen had been held in the spring and summer, to get ready for the next season. I was on the team only because I joined by filling out the application and getting my physical, but I wouldn't officially start practices until the next semester. However, the most important privilege of joining the football team was that at lunchtime you were allowed to sit at the football tables, a section of the cafeteria that was reserved for the football team. Around Christmas time a few of the upperclassmen were harassing freshmen in the cafeteria. My friend Ed was targeted: they made him get up on a lunch table and sing Jingle Bells to everyone in the cafeteria. They told him that if he didn't sing, they would give him a wedgie. The best way to describe a wedgie is when someone forcibly pulls your underwear up from the back of your pants. Poor Ed, with terror in his eyes and shame on his face, started singing and they told him to sing louder. He started crying with his lip quivering, tears streaming down his face, and he kept taking awkward pauses because he was gasping for air and then they gave him a wedgie anyway. You could hear the underwear rip all over the cafeteria. To this day I remember my friend Ed when I hear Jingle Bells. I felt bad for Ed because I couldn't put in a good word for him. I wasn't an active member of the football team and I had absolutely no juice in the school at that point. I was lucky that I wasn't targeted, and it wasn't me up on that table. Times were different back then and even at Brooklyn Tech there was hazing, but that's about as bad as it would get. There actually was not a lot of bullying at the school because everyone, even the upperclassmen, knew how hard the curriculum was and how hard it would be in the coming years. I am glad that the situation has improved today, and the Anti Bullying movement is strong. Growing up as a Latino in New York City is hard enough.

The next semester my schedule became even more hectic because the football team started indoor practices in the winter. Since I had joined the team, I had to earn my stripes. Practices would take place during zero period (before school officially starts), so members of the team had to be there by seven fifteen a.m. I had to leave with my dad in the morning by five thirty a.m. and tag along with him to work. He would drive me to the train station nearest to his job. I was taking the train with construction workers, laborers, medical personnel, bakers and with other people that started their jobs early in the morning. At that time, my dad was part owner of a dental laboratory in Woodside Queens and was working twelve to fourteen hours a day. My mother, who was an administrative assistant for Citibank in the Wall Street area, was also working longer hours. We rarely spent much time together back then, but I understood because my parents had a mortgage and property taxes to pay. I could sense that the entire family was drifting apart. I barely saw my little sister Valeria, who was six years old, but she and I became much closer as she got older. I feel bad because I was an absentee big brother during her early years when in addition to my studies, I had extracurricular activities and worked part-time at a supermarket. Practicing indoors in the winter was grueling: the coaches had us running up and down the stairs all morning. They called it zero period because absolutely zero students wanted to be at school that early. I always liked to run and was very fit, but it was back-breaking running up and down those stairs. Imagine running up and down nine flights of stairs early in the morning before classes started. The custodial staff probably had to be on standby because there were some big dudes on the team sweating buckets all over the stairways. I could imagine students slipping and sliding on their way to their chemistry, physics, and calculus classes. I remember players sometimes throwing up as the coaches ran us ragged up and down those steps. I always wondered why they didn't strategically place buckets on every floor in the stairwell. Those unfortunate custodians were kept busy cleaning up the sweat and the vomit. Imagine a school as big as Tech with an enrollment of five thousand students, and all those students would be slipping and sliding on sweat and vomit on their way to their first period class if the custodians had not been vigilant.

 Once the weather warmed up, the football coaches had us

practicing across the street from the school building, at Fort Greene Park. In my opinion, the famous filmmaker Spike Lee is the best representative of New York City, since he captures the flavor and the pulse of the city. Fort Greene was prominent in Spike Lee's groundbreaking 1986 film *She's Gotta Have It*. He also headquartered his production company, 40 Acres and A Mule Filmworks, in Fort Greene, in the neighborhood where he grew up, which was near our school. Black, Latino or otherwise, Spike Lee represents the essence of what a New Yorker should be better than anyone. I was a diehard New York Knicks Basketball fan back then and I know that he is considered the most famous Knicks fan of all time. If you want to know how much Spike Lee loves the Knicks, check out his movie *Crooklyn* and then you will understand. I saw Spike Lee near the school on a few occasions, but I was never able to talk to him. I was a teenage Latino and I always wanted to act like I was hip and laid back. I wasn't going to start jumping up and down and screaming "Yo, Spike, I love you, man!"

The Brooklyn Tech cheerleading squad appeared in the 1988 Spike Lee film *School Daze*, and a video for the movie, entitled *Da Butt*, was shot at Brooklyn Tech. The cheerleaders were called the Enginettes and the football players were called the Engineers. Those Enginettes used to cheer and dance with incredible energy and spirit – they were great. When I played football for Tech, our team was not very good, but historically Brooklyn Tech has had excellent teams in a competitive New York City Public School Athletic League, despite the high academic standards. Tech was the high school equivalent of universities like Notre Dame and Stanford which are known for strong academics and strong football traditions. During the years that I played football, the cheerleaders saved us from complete embarrassment. I think that fans were more interested in watching the Enginettes do their cheers than in watching us flounder on the football field.

I always appreciated the energy and history in the school building and around the neighborhood while I attended Tech. In the '80s and into the '90s, one of my favorite comedians, Chris Rock, lived in Fort Greene and the famous musician Branford Marsalis and singer Erykah Badu also resided there. I read that one of my favorite writers, Richard Wright, wrote what is considered his best and most famous novel, *Native Son*, while he lived in Fort Greene and the iconic book was written as he enjoyed the trees, foliage, and beauty of Fort Greene Park, several decades before my time there. I went on to read Richard Wright's *Native Son* and *Black Boy* in college and still consider them to be two of the best novels that I have ever read. The neighborhood around the school was residential, with many beautiful brownstone houses, which are rowhouses covered with brown sandstone. It's noteworthy that I lived such a sheltered and insular life in my old neighborhood that I had never even seen a brownstone before I went to Brooklyn Tech. Both Brooklyn and Fort Greene are well-known for their brownstones. The neighborhood as well as the school and the diverse student population opened my eyes to a rich Black culture that changed my life and perspective forever.

Residents from the neighborhood must have thought the football team was crazy for practicing at the park so early in the morning at ungodly hours. The coaches would try to make us work as much as possible until they ended practice by blowing a whistle, whereupon we would all have to run across the street and over to the locker rooms, change clothes and rush to first period. No one had time to shower, and we all barely made it to class on time even without showering. I am sure many students in those classes thought, "Oh no, the football players are coming," because of the strong smells. The coaches always emphasized that we had to be student athletes. Academics were always stressed, and a certain grade point average had to be maintained to remain on the team. By the end of spring, we were all in great shape and we had created a sincere camaraderie as a team. As crazy as it sounds, I miss those insane practices. The demographics of the team were predominantly Black, then white and then a little bit of everything, including Latino and Asian. Even though this might sound disingenuous to an outsider, I can sincerely say that there never were any racial barriers, and we all felt like we were brothers.

Fortunately, I survived my freshman year at Brooklyn Tech. The course work was rigorous, but for the most part, I received good grades, even though I struggled with math. I received A's in my liberal arts courses (including Spanish) and B's in math and science. Of course, my dad complained because I did not get straight A's. Brooklyn Tech was competitive and challenging academically, and it was a tough year for me because my time was occupied by running track, practicing with the football team, doing homework, and commuting to and from school for two hours each way. In the wintertime, it was dark when I left the house in the morning, and then it would be dark again by the time I got home from school.

I didn't have time for a social life and had no time to make friends in my new neighborhood in the suburbs. I started getting comments from my parents like, "Why don't you have a girlfriend?" or "Why don't you have any new friends from the new neighborhood?"

I wanted to scream and say to them, "Do you know what my

schedule is like?" Did they want me to go door to door in my new suburban neighborhood like I was trick or treating during Halloween and ask, "Is there anyone my age that lives here who could be my friend?"

I had to quit the track team, which is one of my big regrets because I was an elite distance runner. I just did not have the time and I did not like the coach because he was never around during practices, and he barely knew who I was. I loved to run so much that I continued running in amateur races and I jogged for miles on end whenever I could. Years later during my honeymoon, I was so excited that while my new wife slept, I ran ten miles in the Mexican heat. Most of the time when I got home after school, all I wanted to do was take a nap. Nevertheless, I remained on the football team, even though I was only five-foot-five and 150 pounds because I loved being on that team.

That summer after my freshman year I went to football camp. Every year during the summer the football team went to a camp in Equinunk, Pennsylvania, to practice. It was like the movie "Remember the Titans," in which all of the Black kids and white kids that were part of the first integrated football team in Virginia back in the early 70s went to training camp in Gettysburg, Pennsylvania and came back as a unified team despite all the racial unrest at the time. Most of us on the team were inner-city kids and money was tight, so we raised money to pay for camp during the year by selling chocolate bars. You would see members of the football team carrying boxes of chocolate bars all over the school. It was a source of pride. I sold most of my chocolate bars to my relatives and family friends. One of the perks of being Latino was having a large extended family.

I looked forward to going to football camp just to get away

from the house. I had not adapted to my new neighborhood, and it had been a grueling year: studying late into the night for exams, reading and doing homework assignments on the train and bus to and from school, and spending countless hours on math and science because they were especially challenging to me. To top it off, I had to put up with being criticized by my father for getting B's in math and science instead of A's. I could not wait to leave for camp that summer. All of us, including the coaches, met at the school, where we would take school buses to Camp Equinunk, in Equinunk, Pennsylvania. Of course, we had to meet at six a.m. We always had to meet early, that would never change. Football coaches, Latino dads, and dads of all cultures are fond of saying, "We have to leave early to avoid the traffic," "We need to get an early start," and "The early bird gets the worm," etc., when all we teenagers want to do is sleep in. That morning there was not a lot of traffic from Brooklyn to Equinunk, so why did we need such an early start? We drove for hours and during the ride, most of the players on the bus were sleeping. We arrived at the camp, and it was in the middle of nowhere. I remember seeing a dead animal on the road to camp that could have been a deer – it was hard to tell – but I knew that we were not in Brooklyn anymore. We went straight out of Brooklyn to Boondocks USA! I think that many of those football players had never seen so much greenery in their lives.

    We were all shown to our living quarters where we would be staying for the next two weeks. We were going to sleep in bunk beds lined up in long wooden cabins, which looked like they were used by the Union army soldiers during the Civil War. Who knows, they looked so old they may have been used during the Revolutionary War. I know I was not the only player thinking that I busted my butt selling all those chocolate bars, just so I could stay here! There was no air conditioning or fans anywhere to be found. The coaches were trying to toughen us up, but this was going a little too far. Apparently, this had been a tradition since the 1940s and Brooklyn Tech had always had successful football teams despite having such high academic standards. There were no arguments about who would get what bunk because they were all equally crappy, so we just picked someone to share our misery. Calling it a bunk bed was an insult to bunk beds. These structures were just two-level, metal frames supporting skinny mattresses that looked like cardboard. I picked a top bunk so that if the rickety springs underneath that meager mattress broke, I'd have someone to land on who would break my fall. Some of our players were big dudes; I still don't know how those bunks held up.

Stupid me, I thought that the coaches would let us relax, settle in, and see the sights on the first day. As soon as we chose our bunk beds and put down our gear, the coaches started blowing their infernal whistles and told us to be on the field in twenty minutes. We had to put on our shoulder pads and equipment and run to the field about half a mile away. Our football gear was old and had been passed down over the years, so it took some time to get used to the strong smells. All of the underclassmen and upperclassmen went to camp together, so we were nearly one hundred young men, sweating profusely in our pads in close proximity to each other. We slept in different cabins, but both the cabins were nasty and decrepit, so there was no preference for either class. I think they did it on purpose to allow the upperclassmen to haze the younger players. All the underclassmen would be placed together in one cabin, ready to be tortured. There were fourteen-year-old kids, practicing with eighteen-year-old men. By then I had experienced my Latino growth spurt, going from five-foot-five to five-foot-six. My dad was five-foot-six, and my mom was five-foot-two, so how tall was I going to be? Brooklyn Tech had a weight room at the school, and it was open to the football team. I started pumping iron during the spring to bulk up for camp and I was now a muscular 155 pounds. I was not exactly a physical specimen.

That's why Latinos generally favor and play soccer, which we call futbol; it has to do with genetics. I didn't care; I loved to play football, not futbol. Instead of Pele, I idolized Joe Namath. I was born in Queens and was a Jets fan. Instead of Maradona, I loved Joe Klecko. Instead of Messie and Ronaldo, I love Patrick Mahomes and Tom Brady. Instead of the World Cup, I wanted to watch the Super Bowl. My parents never understood, so I watched every Super Bowl alone in my room from 1981–1988. No wings, no beer, no nachos, no party, just me alone in my room enjoying the game. That may sound depressing, but now that I go to fancy Super Bowl parties with a lot of non-sports fans that barely watch any football until the Super Bowl, it's hard to enjoy the game. People are more interested in gossiping and eating and drinking. I have seen guests at Super Bowl parties actually getting in the way of the TV screen as if it were a routine cocktail party. I was nineteen years old when I went to my first Super Bowl party. I went to a neighborhood in Brooklyn where my friend James lived, and we watched the game at a bowling alley with his local friends. The beer was flowing, and the wings were all-you-can-eat, and I realized that I had been missing out on all the fun, including a chance to talk sports with the guys. I was a sports junkie since I was about eight years old and it felt good to show off my sports trivia knowledge in a group. James was on the football team, and we became good friends. He was at camp with me that summer. He looked like a good athlete, tall and strong, but he was too slow. He looked like Tarzan but played like Jane. James mother was Irish and his father was Puerto Rican, so he looked like a white boy.

That summer at Camp Equinunk, my bunkmate was Charly. He was a short, skinny Jewish kid from Forest Hills, Queens. Charly was my size and I wondered if he would make the cut. The first day that I saw him run, he ran like a gazelle; I never saw a white kid run that fast. I was fast but my speed was not explosive like that. I was a long-distance runner who started out fast and got even faster the longer I ran. Soon Charly and I became great buddies, so I introduced Charly to my friend James, and the three of us formed a friendship that would last throughout high school. Once we hit the field everyone saw how fast Charly was, and he gained everyone's respect immediately. When I found out that I loved to hit people, I became a tackling machine during practice. I was tackling everyone big, small, tall; it didn't matter, I was going to attack them. Most of the team was Black. I honestly never felt any animosity, or what might be called reverse racism against those of us who were fair skinned, since we were all going through hell at camp, and we were doing it as brothers. I also met one of my soon-to-be friends Yusef, who was my size but skinnier, if that's possible. He had to be the skinniest kid in the whole camp, but I truly believe he had the biggest heart on the entire team because he worked harder than anyone, underclassmen or upperclassmen, bar none. It does not surprise me that Yusef went on to work as an engineer for the National Aeronautics and Space Administration (NASA).

Latino, Black, white, Jewish, it didn't matter, the coaches treated us all equally the same: like cockroaches! Yelling, screaming, grabbing our facemasks… It was all tough love, and we all grew to love the coaches. Three practices a day in the hot sun in full pads, classroom sessions in the evening, and wind sprints to end practices: coach blows the whistle, you run until he blows the whistle again, then you stop. Then the pattern is repeated over and over again! Those wicked whistles still give me nightmares. Sports are the great equalizer; if more kids participated in sports and joined sports teams, it would help tear down racial barriers more than all the rhetoric and posturing that goes on. Everyone is enthusiastic about change during times of crisis, as people pour out into the streets and express their outrage after tragedies such as the beating of Rodney King and the killing of George Floyd. Unfortunately, as time passes by, many people lose interest and move on to the next cause. Racism is systemic and is passed down from generation to generation. Being part of a team and training and competing with teammates that you respect regardless of skin color or ethnicity helps to break the vicious cycle.

My parents had said that Blacks and Latinos do not get along and I would understand when I got older. Actually, I respected the Black culture even more after that summer. If you get enough people like me breaking that vicious cycle, then perhaps our kids and grandkids could help make a significant change. Of course, there were some misinformed white and Black parents who were telling their kids to stay away from Latinos because of negative stereotypes such as: Latinos spread AIDS, sell drugs and cheat on their partners; they are thieves, illegal aliens and wetbacks; they are in gangs or on welfare, and cannot be trusted. The reason I am mentioning these awful stereotypes is throughout my years growing up as a Latino in New York City, they were either said directly to me or about me. It is essential that we get to know people by their character and not the color of their skin or their ethnicity. The problem is that Latinos and Blacks in this country are not afforded the same privileges as whites. Funding for schools in minority neighborhoods is unequal, funding for books is unequal, treatment by law enforcement is unequal. A white man or woman will never have to worry about being shot by a police officer or murdered during a simple traffic stop. The same cannot be said for minorities in this country.

I came home that summer feeling like I could conquer the world. Then my parents started pestering me again because I didn't have any friends in the neighborhood, and I didn't have a girlfriend. I had a lot of new friends, but they lived all over the city, and I didn't have a car or money to travel to all the areas where my new friends lived. I could not wait for the beginning of the fall term when I would become a starter for the junior varsity football team, and I could sit at the football table with pride. I had school friends now and I felt more comfortable in my own skin.

Nonetheless, the commute to school every day was a killer. Two hours each way from Bayside, Queens to Fort Greene, Brooklyn. Brooklyn in the 1980s was different from what it is today. By the time I started my sophomore year at Tech, the crack epidemic was exploding. There was a lot of crime and violence all over New York City, including Brooklyn. The classic movie *New Jack City*, with Wesley Snipes playing the notorious Nino Brown character, was New York City's version of Miami's *Scarface*, with Al Pacino playing the ruthless Tony Montana. Fort Greene was primarily a residential middle-class neighborhood. When we were at school we were insulated and generally safe. Once school was over, however, all bets were off. The bordering neighborhoods included Bedford-Stuyvesant, East New York, Brownsville, Bushwick and Williamsburg, considered to be some of the most dangerous in the world during the '80s. Back then, the only train that would go directly from Brooklyn to Queens was the G Train. The Fulton Street G train station was half a block from the school, but that route could be risky. If I wanted to take another subway train home after school, I could take the N Train at the Dekalb Avenue train stop in downtown Brooklyn. It was over half a mile away from Tech, plus it went through Manhattan before it got to Queens. So, if I took the N train, I would have to travel through two boroughs just to get to Queens, which would add another half hour to my commute. In the 1980s, over two hundred and fifty felony crimes were committed every week in the New York City subway system, and it was considered the most dangerous mass transit system in the world. Taking the G train very early in the morning was never an issue, since criminals, pickpockets, predators, and thugs generally don't get up early in the morning. Their work usually starts after noon and gets busier after dark. You would think that the Fulton Street G train station would be well protected, as students from one of the most prestigious high schools in the country took that train every day and deserved to be kept safe. During all the time that I rode the G train while I went to Tech, I never saw a police officer.

One day during my sophomore year, I met up with my friend Charly after school and took the G train home. We were waiting on the platform and two older guys approached us. They were taller and bigger than us and I knew they were not high school students. I grew up in a tough neighborhood and hung out with a lot of hardcore criminal types when I was young. I knew that being a hardcore criminal has nothing to do with color or ethnicity; criminals have a hardened look and their eyes appear blank and soulless. The person shows no compassion or feeling and seems to have a black heart. Nobody is born like that; usually, it has to do with a history of abuse or a rough upbringing. I became a criminal prosecutor later in life and I found that the worst repeat offenders had that look. The older guy that approached us at the G train station that day had that look. I believed that I was tough, and I grew up in a rough neighborhood, so I stood my ground. My instincts told me to run but I did not want to be perceived as a punk. I never had any money in those days, so I wasn't that worried about what they might take from me. Then I realized I was wearing the gold chain that my mom brought me from Colombia when I was a kid. It had a pendant with the Virgin Mary and an inscription *Que dios te bendiga hijo* (May God bless you son). My mother, María del Carmen, was named after the Virgin Mary. She told me to wear the chain for protection so that the Virgin Mary could look over me. Before I could react, that thug put me in a chokehold. I was stunned and I froze. To this day I wonder why I didn't fight back. Maybe they had weapons, and I could have been killed, who knows? It all happened very quickly: after he put me in the choke hold his friend snatched the chain from my neck and they both took off. It was over in a matter of seconds. I was not hurt, but I felt embarrassed. Charly was in shock. It happened so fast, there was nothing he could have done to help me.

When I got home, I cried because I felt that I had let my mother down. She bought that chain and pendant for me for my protection and with love and I let those thugs snatch it from my neck. She immediately told me that she was not disappointed and was happy that I did not try to do anything because I could have been hurt or killed; she gave me a hug and told me that my safety came first before any material things and that she loved me. After that I vowed never to take the G train unless I had a group of friends with me; if not, I would walk to Dekalb Avenue and take the N train. I was angry that I had to do that, especially during the winter months. Sometimes I saw some Tech students getting their electronic equipment stolen at the G train station. The Walkman was popular then, as well as some other electronic devices; not like today, but the electronic revolution was beginning. I believe that bad kids from other schools and criminals from other neighborhoods would target that train station. A lot of Asian Tech students who lived in Queens took the G train; I cannot count how many Asian kids I saw mugged at the Fulton Street G train station during my time at Tech. Despite all the robberies and violence, there never was a police presence.

  The worst mugging, I have ever seen in my life happened at that Fulton Street G train station, in the early evening. An older Asian couple, who looked Japanese, walked into the train station at the Fulton Street G stop. I thought they were tourists because they looked lost. The woman was wearing a white mink coat, and her companion was wearing a nice suit with a wool coat. The Brooklyn Academy of Music was near Brooklyn Tech, so perhaps they were trying to get back to their hotel after a show. The Brooklyn Academy of Music put on a lot of great shows and is a historic venue in downtown Brooklyn. I don't know if they were being followed, but once they went through those train station turnstiles a posse of teenagers came rushing into the station, jumping over the turnstiles. It looked like the train booth operator conveniently decided to take a break. I was with a few friends, but we were not getting involved because the posse was deep, and they acted like a pack of wolves. One of the guys put the woman in a chokehold and lifted her off the ground. I heard loud screams; she was gasping for air, and I heard blood-curdling gurgling sounds. I was terrified and I thought that he may have killed that innocent woman. The other kids started stripping her of all her belongings: her purse, her mink coat, her jewelry, and anything of value she had on her. The man she was with was beaten down and could not do anything to help her. They took his wallet and any jewelry that he had on him. Where were the police? Just one officer at the station would have prevented this atrocity. Once those hapless tourists were stripped of all their belongings, the posse scurried off and disappeared. It all happened in a matter of minutes. There were some adult bystanders that came to help after it was over. Commuters had to yell at the booth clerk to call the police because there were no cell phones back then.

Later that year the Brooklyn Tech basketball team was attacked while riding on the G train on their way to a basketball game at another school. A gang approached them on the subway train and told them to give up their valuables. The coach was with them and as an adult authority figure he told them to leave, or he would call the police. One of the gang members pulled out a gun and they took a sheepskin coat from one of the players. In those days sheepskin coats were popular and expensive, so that basketball player probably got his sheepskin coat as a gift or had to work long hours at a part-time job to buy it. Just like that, they took it and ran off. That basketball player was my friend, and I knew exactly how he felt.

After my chain was stolen, I started carrying a knife that I had bought at a shop in the old neighborhood. I had a collection of knives because I liked them and used to collect them as a hobby. I had hunting knives, switch blades, martial arts knives and other knives that I bought at that shop. After I was mugged, I used to put one in my school bag, and nobody knew. Back then there were no metal detectors at the schools in New York City like there are today. Around the same time period, a few days before Christmas back in 1984, Bernhard Goetz shot four young inner-city youths on a New York City subway car. Apparently, he was out to shoot would-be muggers because he had been the victim of a mugging. Later the news came out that the four youths were unarmed. He shot all of them anyway. The worst part of his statement to the press was that he wanted to murder them and make them suffer and his regret was that he ran out of bullets. After wounding three of the youths, Bernard Goetz pointed his gun at eighteen-year-old Darrel Cabey, who hadn't been wounded but was cowering in the subway car. Goetz shot him in the back, paralyzing him for life and causing brain damage. The shooting appeared to be racially motivated. Were the boys going to mug him? Maybe. Did they deserve to be shot, and did an eighteen-year-old deserve to be paralyzed for life over a couple of bucks? No! I stopped carrying my knife because either I would use it and potentially kill someone, or I would get myself killed. Violence was not the answer, especially over a few dollars or material possessions. In an ironic twist, the G train line is now considered one of the hippest train lines in New York City, and Brooklyn has transformed into one of the hippest places to live. Actors, writers, poets, artists, and everyone who is anyone lives in Brooklyn. The popular HBO series *Girls* (2012–2017) featured actress Lena Dunham playing struggling writer Hannah Horvath, who lived near the G train and took the train at the Greenpoint stop. Today hipsters take the G train, and no one is being mugged or getting shot. However, now that Brooklyn has been gentrified and is a hip place to live, there is a police presence at every G train stop.

In the fall semester of my junior year, I started hanging out with what I call the weed crew, and I spent more and more time with them as the year progressed. Most of the kids grew up in tough neighborhoods and were inner-city kids but were smart and always did well in school without trying. They were all part of the counterculture and were considered misfits at Tech, and that's why I gravitated toward them. To underscore the diversity of the school, the racial breakdown of the weed crew was white, Black, Latino, Arabic, West Indian, Jamaican and Greek. From social media and from what I have heard, many members of the weed crew have respectable jobs now or are very successful entrepreneurs; some have found success in the music and entertainment industries. That junior year, one of the guys in the weed crew borrowed a key from the school custodian (I say he borrowed it because if you steal something you don't give it back). The key was to the door that led to the school roof, a perfect place to smoke weed. He had a copy made and put it back before the custodian ever noticed it was missing. I don't know where my friend had a copy of that key made so quickly; I wonder if he made it himself in one of the machine shops or in the school's foundry. Tech had a lot of elaborate equipment.

When the regulars of the weed crew didn't have their usual stashes, we would go to weed spots near the school, like going to a bank teller. You would knock on what looked like a wooden window or square in some storefront or decrepit apartment building and someone would ask, "How much?" We bought as much as we could by pooling our lunch money together. By then I had smoked weed here and there for a couple of years, but I never had learned how to roll a joint. Most of the time we would buy Philly blunt cigars from the corner bodega on Fulton Street near the school, empty out the tobacco and fill it with marijuana. Back in the day, we used to smoke some strong stuff. I even took my Chemistry Regents Exam high. At Tech you had to pass the New York State Regents Exam in every subject in order to pass the class, even though that was not required in most other high schools. A Regents diploma is what most high school students strive for but fail to achieve. At Tech it was required. When I opened my test booklet the questions appeared to be jumping off the pages. It's hard to complete multiple-choice questions when the letters are moving around. Predictably, I barely passed the exam. Chemistry was one of my favorite classes and I had done well all year. Instead of a 90, my grade was lowered to an 85. I was disappointed because I felt like I let down one of my favorite teachers, my chemistry teacher Mr. Black. I never smoked as much as the others and half the time I just did it to try to fit in. I lost my taste for it after that and stopped smoking weed. Today marijuana is not taboo in the mainstream the way it was in the 1980s. Marijuana laws have been relaxed in almost all the states, and it is hip to smoke pot now. My dad never knew that I smoked pot; if he had found out back then, he would have killed me.

    Mr. Black, my chemistry teacher, was my favorite teacher while I was at Brooklyn Tech. Everyone always has a favorite teacher in high school. Never in a million years would I ever think that Mr. Black would be my favorite teacher at Tech. I always had to work harder when it came to math and science because these subjects did not come easy to me. I always joke about becoming an attorney because I hated math and science. Mr. Black made me look forward to learning about chemistry. Everyone in my class was eager to attend chemistry class. We were a diverse group, and he had no favorites; he treated us all equally badly. He used to love to give us all a hard time but in a playful way. There was a lot of give and take and he was very sarcastic. He was a tall, dorky-looking, middle-aged white man who wore glasses and a long white lab coat. I remember during one class he pulled out a giant thermometer. He asked the class, "Does anyone know what this is?" Students raised their hands and tried to give intelligent answers because we were the best of the best after all. He shot everyone down: "No, No, No!" Finally, he asked, "Do you all give up?"

The whole class groaned and said "Yes, we give up!"

Then he declared, "This is called a rectum finder! For all those science enthusiasts out there, the technical term for a rectum, if you don't already know, is the final section of the large intestine, terminating at the anus." We all cracked up hysterically. Now if you think that story is disturbing or sick, then now you know why we all loved Mr. Black.

Mr. Black was always conducting fun and interesting experiments. One afternoon he conducted an experiment that dealt with neutralizing acidic materials. He showed the class a small raw jalapeño pepper and asked if anyone would eat the raw pepper in front of the classroom for extra credit. I was Latino and the pepper looked tiny. I had never had a raw jalapeño pepper before but how hot could it be? I ran up and put it in my mouth. I was going to get my extra credit and make Mr. Black look bad (see, no big deal). Then I started to feel a burning sensation and my eyes starting tearing. With a wry smile, Mr. Black asked me, "Mr. Ossa, are you okay?"

Finally, I couldn't take it anymore and I ran out of the classroom looking for a sink so that I could drink water. I finally drank some water, but it didn't help. When I got back to class everyone was laughing hysterically. Then Mr. Black handed me a glass of milk that he had hidden behind his back. He then explained the reaction and the soothing effect of the milk. I thought it was funny and he kept his word and gave me extra credit. During other experiments or the trivia games that Mr. Black had us play to help us learn chemistry, the class would get so riled up that school security guards would come to the classroom to make sure everything was okay, or to tell us to quiet down because other teachers were complaining.

On March 5, 1985, we heard screaming outside of the classroom and we all thought it was just students goofing around. Mr. Black commented that finally some of the other teachers had seen the light and were using his teaching methods. The screaming died down, then it became scary because it was eerily silent. Mr. Black went outside and never came back. The class was dismissed early by another teacher, and later we found out that a teacher at Tech, Mrs. T, had been stabbed four times by asixteen-year-old student. . Mr. Black helped her, and she was taken to the hospital and survived the attack. Even inside the specialized high school, we were not shielded from the violence that plagued New York City in the 1980s. Mr. Robert Black retired years later and became a famous inventor. He is a multimillionaire and has over sixteen patents. He delayed his riches because he loved teaching kids. All New York City schools should have teachers like Mr. Black.

After a second summer at football camp, I had made the varsity football team and was looking forward to playing in the fall of my junior year. A week before our first game, I tackled another player during practice and landed awkwardly on the hard, rock-filled field. Since we did not have our own field, the team had to practice a few blocks away from Tech, at Sterling High School. When I got up after making that tackle during practice, I felt extreme pain in my left wrist. When I looked at my wrist, I wanted to faint. My usually strong, straight wrist had gone limp, like spaghetti. My hand was just dangling from my arm, like a yo-yo stuck at the bottom of its string. I had never broken a bone before, and I knew it was a serious injury. One of the coaches took me to the hospital, where X-rays were taken, and I was diagnosed with a comminuted wrist fracture (broken into several pieces). On my left arm they put a hard plaster cast that extended all the way up to my elbow. The doctor told me very solemnly that my season was over. When my parents came to pick me up at the hospital, I was crying hysterically. My pain threshold was always high, and I had been given painkillers. I wasn't crying because of any pain; I was crying because I had worked so hard for two years to make the varsity team. I had gone to school early in the mornings for winter and spring practices and stayed late in the fall during the football season. I attended tutoring to keep my grades up in math to stay on the football team. I wore my football jersey with pride, and I even bought a Brooklyn Tech Engineer Football jacket. I had sold chocolate bars, attended two summer camps, started for the junior varsity team during my sophomore year, practiced for two winters and two springs, survived all the blood, sweat and tears that it took to balance being on the team with getting good grades and now my brief football career was over, just like that! As a five-foot-six, 155-pound Latino cornerback, I knew that I wouldn't get a college football scholarship and I didn't have any dreams of making the NFL, but I just loved to play. I loved to lift weights with the guys, practice with the guys, run with the guys and I loved the camaraderie of being part of the team. Just like that, football was taken away from me.

It felt like a new beginning because I was no longer on the football team, so after my wrist healed, I finally had time to venture into my new neighborhood and I found new friends. At that age, I got around on my bicycle and would ride for miles looking for handball games. I started playing handball in the old neighborhood when I was a kid. Handball is the ultimate inner-city sport. It is like tennis, except you use your hands to hit a ball against a wall, and you have serves, aces, volleys and points. There is a lot of strategy involved when playing handball and you can play singles or doubles. It was cheap to play, since all you needed was a handball, usually a blue rubber ball like the one used for indoor racquetball. There is a sport called team handball that is played in Europe and the Olympics, but it is nothing like street handball. If you look in any hood in New York City, you will always see kids and adults playing handball. Street handball is played by people of all ethnicities, but it is predominantly a minority sport. Usually, Latinos and Blacks are the best players in the city. If the inner-city and minorities in New York City had to have an official sport, an argument can be made that it would be handball, even over baseball and basketball.

The great thing about handball is that it created a diversion for minority youths like me. No matter how bad the neighborhood, I never saw any fights or violence at a handball court. Nobody was getting shot, nobody was getting robbed, nobody was getting harassed; you would just see everyone playing, watching, and admiring the crazy skills that some of these players had. The handball court was a safe haven for everyone, players and spectators alike. All you had to do when on the court was call "next" and wait until it was your turn to play. No one would mess with you; if you were good, you won and kept playing. I believe that handball courts served as a summer camp for minority kids whose immigrant parents, single moms or grandmas could not afford to pay for camp. I can't imagine growing up without playing handball. Usually on a weekend the courts would get crowded, so most games had to be doubles games. It would get so crowded and loud that you thought you were at a baseball game in a small stadium. The only thing that was missing was a vendor yelling "Hot dogs here!" or "Beer here!" You could bring a friend to be your partner, or you could hook up with someone at the courts who needed a partner.

When I was a kid in the old neighborhood, I played at a park in East Elmhurst near my junior high school during the summer. I called "next" and was waiting to play. The park was crowded, and I needed a partner so I could play doubles. I was sitting and waiting, hoping that someone would show up who could be my partner. I saw an older Latino man come to the court and he was wearing a shiny, silver, silk dress shirt, tight black dress pants and shiny black patent leather dress shoes. He had no neck, and he was a big, stocky, downright scary-looking dude! He asked me in a loud deep voice "Yo, who got next?"

I said, "me" as I gulped.

He then asked, "Do you need a partner?"

I sheepishly said yes, and he agreed to play with me. I was about twelve years old, and I was talking to a scary looking, grown man. He looked like he could be my dad's age. He told me that he was just released from prison and that he was wearing the same clothes he had on when he went in. He came straight to the park because he felt that he had gained too much weight while inside and wanted to get a game before he got home and saw his girlfriend and his kid later that day. He wanted to surprise them because he received an early release. I thought he was strange, but I got past that, and we played next and won ten games in a row. I had to leave because I had to get home before my curfew, or my dad would kill me. My new friend understood. He told me,

"I am a pops, too!" He thanked me and said "good-lookin' little man," which in the old neighborhood is another way of saying thank you. I didn't find anything strange about that day, it was just another summer day in the hood!

On any given weekend I would see people of all ages and ethnicities playing handball. If you were good and had game, that's all you needed. I spent many weekends just biking around all over the city looking for games. I could go to a park for the first time and spend the whole day playing handball. I had a small following because when you get good, people start getting to know you. Players even hustled for money. Over the years I played handball against high school students, college students, senior citizens, stockbrokers, doctors, lawyers, ex-convicts, drug dealers, hardcore criminals, cops, construction workers, you name it, I played against them or with them. There were famous parks where handball was played all over the city, but the Yankee Stadium of handball parks was on West 4th Street in Greenwich Village. The courts were located at the corner of West 4th Street and Sixth Avenue/Avenue of the Americas. In New York City back in the day, all those who thought they were good handball players had to prove themselves at West 4th Street. There were a lot of money games. I played there and all over the city. I liked to play in Queens and stay close to home. Every park that was known for handball had a top dog, a champion. To this day everyone thinks they were the best. It is a total testosterone-driven game. Now that I am working as a trial attorney in New York City, it reminds me of the whole handball scene. Everyone talks a good game until they get their butts kicked. The reality is there is always someone better. Every time you think you're the best, you run into someone that's better.

On the other side of the tracks, near the border of Bayside

where I lived and the neighboring town Francis Lewis, I finally found a park that I could call home. I felt comfortable around the Blacks, Latinos and other people who gathered there. I guess there is some truth to the saying that you can take the Latino out of the hood, but you can't take the hood out of the Latino. I made several new Latino friends. Elvin and Luis were both Colombians whose parents had recently moved to the United States seeking better opportunities. Elvin would end up becoming a banker, Luis became an engineer and their sister Gabby became a doctor. Also, they had a friend Jerry, who was from Venezuela and his dad was a diplomat. I met them at the handball courts at the park, which was only about a mile away from my house, but culturally (Good) it felt like it was 100 miles away. There were young minorities who hung out at the park, and I enjoyed talking with and relating to them. There was always hip-hop music blasting and there were a lot of minority children at the park. There were a few group homes nearby, with foster kids that came from impoverished homes. It was not the hood where I grew up, but it was a place where I could feel comfortable. When I first went to the park, I saw kids playing handball. I called "next" and proceeded to win every game. There were some young teenage girls that were checking me out that day. I was beating everyone in the park, and it made me feel good. After I had been playing for hours, someone called the local legend Rakim to come play me. I was about to leave because it was getting late and then Rakim showed up. He was a Black man in his late twenties, and he was wearing overalls that were full of paint stains. He was a painter and had just come home after work when he got the call. I was eager to whip the local legend's butt in front of all the pretty young girls.

When Rakim saw me, he said, "That's it! You sorry asses

called me to play this kid?" I was so ready to teach that arrogant bastard a lesson! When we started playing, he let me serve first. I aced him and everyone was oohing and ahhing in amazement. Rakim just smiled, took off his T-shirt and undid the top of his overalls. He was chiseled: he had a six pack and muscles upon muscles. He started stretching his legs and arms and cracking his neck, then he said, "Okay, now I'm ready."

I thought to myself, "I don't care what you do and how much you show off, I am going to kick your ass in front of your home crowd." There must have been at least a hundred people watching. I tried to ace him again, but he was not having it. Rakim was ambidextrous and was hitting killers and rollers with both hands. A killer is when you hit the ball so low to the ground that it rolls off the wall and is indefensible. He had a killer serve that exploded off his fist. I have to admit, he was the best player I had ever seen. I was the one who got my ass kicked, but after that, we became great friends. He was a lot older than me and became a mentor to me. We talked about life and girls and more importantly, we became doubles partners. It would take me two years to finally beat Rakim. I would not play him in a singles game until I felt that I was good enough. I began practicing with my left hand, since I was righthanded. I even played kids with my left hand only. It became an obsession, even though Rakim and I were friends and played doubles together and beat the pants off everybody we played. People would come from other neighborhoods and Rakim and I would smoke everyone. Back in those days that park was always rockin'! There was gang activity and drugs being sold in the park, but nobody ever messed with me or Rakim. It was my park and I had respect from all the local gangsters.

Years later when I was studying for the LSAT (the Law

School Admission Test, like the SAT for college), I would go to that same park and play handball to unwind and let off steam after hours of studying. One day I called Rakim on a Saturday morning and I told him I was ready.

He said, "Are you ready to get your ass kicked again?"

I said, "Sure, why not?"

He even volunteered to spot me a few points, but he wanted to play for money. I said no because I never liked to play for money. I never liked gambling, even to this day. He showed up and we began to play. There was no one there to watch this time because it was so early in the morning. Since the last time we played together, I had played alone at hundreds of different parks and practiced for hours. Rakim knew I was getting better at doubles, but he had no idea how good I had become at singles. The game was tight, and it seemed like we played for hours. With my fingertips I was picking up every killer that he tried to throw at me. I was running and diving like a maniac all over the court, picking up his ace serves and his line drive volleys. I was using both hands, which surprised him. Finally, I won the game 21-19. It was one of my proudest accomplishments ever! Rakim was a grown man with a crappy job, and he had kids to support with different mothers. I beat him for me, but I had no interest in taking away his title of King of the Park because I knew it meant a lot to him. We never played against each other after that and we never spoke about that day again, but we continued beating everyone up in doubles games.

I saw him years later and I asked him if he remembered that day when I beat him. He laughed and winked at me and said, "You never beat me. Where are your witnesses?" Sometime later, Rakim stopped coming to the park. I never found out what happened to him, and I missed his friendship.

I started seeing a pretty girl at the park playing handball; her name was Linda and she used to come to the park with her sister Stacy. She was my age and she lived across the street from the park. She looked athletic and wore baggy, comfortable clothes. We became friendly but I didn't think about dating her or anything like that. One day in the early spring of 1986, she asked me out and said she wanted to be my girlfriend. She was a strawberry blond, very fair-skinned and was Scottish/Italian. She liked playing handball and she was pretty good at it, plus she was easy on the eyes. All this was very unexpected. My parents had been harassing me for years about why I didn't have a girlfriend. My schedule was hectic, and I didn't know anyone in the new neighborhood. What did they want from me? They were asking me if I was a homosexual. Seriously, Mom and Dad! I have no idea what they were thinking. Latino parents can be so negative and homophobic. I happily said yes to Linda. However, I was working part-time at the fast-food restaurant White Castle and, between work and going to school, I barely had time for any social life. I was always broke, so where would I take my new girlfriend on dates?

For our first official date, I picked her up at her house, where she was waiting for me on the front porch. Her mother was a single mom and rented a second-floor apartment in a two-family house. Her mother was Italian and her father, who lived in another state, was Scottish. Linda had not seen him since she was a little girl, and he was not involved in her upbringing. Linda, her mom and her sister struggled financially and the house where they lived was old and dilapidated. I was never invited into her home, and I rarely saw or spoke to her mother the entire time we dated. Linda's mother did not approve of our relationship because I was Latino.

When I picked Linda up on our first date, she was wearing a form-fitting skirt and a tight blouse, with flat white shoes. She was a little taller than me and likely did not want me to be embarrassed by her wearing heels. She wore makeup and tied her hair back in a ponytail. She was pretty and had a nice body. I had always seen her with baggy clothes and without makeup, so I was pleasantly surprised, and I was smitten. I was sixteen and did not have a driver's license or access to a car, so our first date would have to be on foot. We walked to the local convenience store, and I bought Boones Island wine coolers and paper cups. At that time, the convenience store by the park did not ask for or require ID. The drinking age was twenty-one, but the rules were not strictly enforced back in the day. In retrospect, that first date was very "ghetto fabulous," but we were just kids and were happy to be spending time together. We walked back to the park where we first met, sat on a park bench, and sipped our wine coolers in paper cups under the stars. There were drug transactions going on and I thought I heard a few gun shots but I knew nobody at the park would mess with me, and we were like the royal couple of the park. We gazed into each other's eyes and kissed under the moonlit sky. We talked and cuddled for hours. It felt good to kiss her and hold her body; we were compatible. I enjoyed her scent. There is a saying that animals know they are compatible by the pheromones they secrete. That's why couples talk about the smell of an absent lover's clothing when they are missed. We had to end our date because Linda had a curfew, and her mother was strict. I could not kiss her good night when we got to her home because her mother was looking out the window.

Linda and I talked on the phone every day and were hanging out as much as we could. It was hard to see her because I was going to school in Brooklyn and working part-time. Between my prolonged commute and my hectic schedule, I was barely able to see her. After a few weeks, we were saying that we loved each other. We were just kids, and we didn't know what love was. I got tired of taking her for walks; it stopped being romantic after a while, so I brought her to my house and introduced her to my family. My mom and my abuelitas were cordial but were not thrilled because she was not Latina. My dad looked at her like a prisoner on death row looks at a steak when he's having his last meal. It was a little awkward that my dad looked like he was hot for my girlfriend. He told me that she was attractive and congratulated me. That was the first compliment he had given me in years.

  My dad and I were fighting like cats and dogs back then. I was losing my luster in his eyes, and I could sense his disappointment because he felt that I was no longer a prodigy. I was doing well at Tech but not at an elite level like he expected and wanted. I was no longer receiving straight A's the way I used to, and A's and B's were just not good enough to get into an Ivy League School. I was starting to think about not continuing at Tech. During my junior year I was taking physics, and my teacher had a heavy accent and was hard to understand. He was brilliant but he didn't seem to care, he was just collecting a paycheck. After having the best science teacher ever, Mr. Black, I tuned out this new teacher. My trigonometry professor did not care for me, and there may have been some racism involved. I was smoking a cigarette with some friends (a bad habit I picked up) and my math teacher saw me outside of school. The next day in front of the whole class he proclaimed, "Mr. Ossa, I saw you smoking marijuana outside with your friends yesterday." I did not do anything to provoke him to say such a thing. I was embarrassed and thought he was offensive and inappropriate. I was angry and wanted to retaliate, but I knew better. What recourse did I have? He had already sent me to the dean's office for alleged inappropriate behavior in class on multiple occasions, while letting off the hook the other students who were equally at fault for making playful remarks. I felt that he was unfairly targeting me, and I had no one to consult about this. I couldn't say anything to my father because he would just tune me out or try to blame me and punish me. I didn't feel comfortable going to the dean's office because he would take the teacher's side. I just stopped going to his class, which was the dumbest thing I could have done, but I felt like I had no choice. I was struggling with my engineer modeling and technical drawing classes. I did not have the skill set or aptitude to excel in these classes. I found out fairly quickly that I would never become or want to become an engineer. I was bartering with my football buddy Sam; he would do my technical drawing assignments and projects and I would do his English assignments, essays, and book reports. This arrangement was not sustainable because there would be in-class exams and assignments. I was even feuding with my Spanish teacher because he was awful and incompetent. "Mr. C" was well versed in Spanish as he was a native speaker, but his English left a lot to be desired. Some of his translations were off and he did not appreciate being corrected. Despite getting 100's on my exams he would lower my grade for alleged subversive behavior. Was it just me? Was I fulfilling a prophecy of what society expected from a young Latino in America? I was at one of the lowest points in my young life.

    I felt alienated from my parents and alone in the world. My new girlfriend Linda was the only one I trusted. It's unfortunate that when kids become teenagers many feel that no one understands them. Is it a lack of communication with their parents? Or the hormones that make them feel out of control? Is it a realization that the real world is right around the corner? Could it be a rite of passage, or an expression of frustration for being misunderstood and not having an identity? I find that old-school parents – perhaps even new-school parents – just don't want to deal with the challenges. You will hear the following from many old-school immigrant parents: "I put the food on the table! I'm breaking my back at work every day! Stop being an ungrateful brat and do your part! You are lucky that you have a roof over your head! Your sister/brother did not cause me these problems!" Any outsider would agree with the adults. However, the teenage years are a difficult stage in a child's development to navigate. Kids are developing an identity and deserve some respect, patience, guidance, and help, instead of disrespect, impatience, anger, and scorn. As of today, my father has never told me that he loved me, ever! That would probably be a step in the right direction. Parents make a conscious decision to have children. Whether they are married or not, whether the child is born out of wedlock, whether the child was an accident, whether the father freaked out and did not take responsibility, once that baby comes into this world, a conscious decision is made.

When babies are born, they are cute and adorable. We all know that it requires a lot of hard work to raise kids. However, when they are old enough to have an opinion, I believe that it's a parent's job to listen. I believe children deserve unconditional love because they did not make the conscious decision to be brought into this world. So many old-school parents believe that teenagers are all irresponsible and should be tolerated but generally ignored. Many parents believe that when their kids become adults, they will see how great their parents were and how good they – the kids – had it. Immigrant parents will declare that they had it worse in their countries and that their kids are disrespectful, ungrateful brats that don't understand or appreciate how good they have it. That may be the case, but why give up on your kids and wait until they become adults? Why not get actively involved in their lives at the moment when they need the most help and encouragement? You may get cursed or yelled at, but you have to put your big boy or big girl pants on and be responsible adults. For a lot of minority and inner-city kids, these are the crucial years when their future hangs in the balance.

As a broader illustration of life in the hood, here are examples of choices made by kids that I grew up with or have known over the years. In each of these scenarios, the wrong choices were made with dire consequences. Drop out of school, because I am making more money selling drugs than my own teachers and parents. Date that drug dealer boyfriend because he is the only one that understands me, and he buys me nice things. Join that gang because unlike my family, they truly care about me, have my back and are my real family. Drop out of school because it is a waste of time, and I can make money right away and leave the house. Keep having babies with that boyfriend who does not have a job but truly loves me. Keep doing drugs because they make me feel good and I have it under control. Date that married guy because he will leave his wife and he truly loves me. Stay with that toxic girlfriend and turn my back on my family because she is the love of my life and is the only one that understands me. Hide my sexuality and remain in the closet because otherwise I will lose my family's love. Don't tell my parents that I am pregnant and have an abortion at an unhygienic and unsafe clinic. Run away from home because I hate my family and I feel like I have no other choices. Take my life because I feel alone in the world and when I die my parents will finally understand how much I was hurting. Looking at the above choices which have been made by countless teenagers over the years, as a parent I would rather be disrespected, embarrassed and seen as weak rather than have my beloved kids make these disastrous choices. Easier said than done for many parents!

Even after tireless efforts, sometimes it's not enough, but at least you could feel that you did everything you could to save your child. As a parent, instead of spending the rest of my life wondering what I might have done wrong, I could set aside my ego, take a different perspective, modify my expectations, and do what I have to do to show my children that I will be there for them unconditionally. There is a famous book about teenage suicide named *13 Reasons Why* that was published in 2007 and became a Netflix drama series. It has been widely popular and has raised awareness of teenage suicide. As a parent today I want to be able to say that I made at least 13,000,000 attempts to help my daughters before they even thought about taking their lives. Sometimes depression and mental illness cannot be handled by motherly or fatherly advice, but as a parent it is our job to recognize when intervention, counseling and/or medical help is needed. As far as I am concerned, as a father my job is not over until the day that I die and even then, God willing, if I can I will look after my kids from above.

CHAPTER 10

There is a timeworn saying "If I knew then what I know now…" which applies to this part of the story. My girlfriend Linda did not like attending the local school, Bayside High, and she just wanted to get a full-time job, move out of her house and be independent as soon as possible. I sympathized because she grew up in a tough situation with a single mom, but I felt that it was shortsighted thinking and I often talked to her about going to college. However, for the moment all we wanted to do was spend time together. She wanted to take our relationship to the next level. She told me that she was a virgin and she wanted to make love to me. We came up with a plan to skip school and go to my house after my parents left for work and my little sister went to school. My Abuelita Aura and my Abuelita Hortencia would be home, but I would tell them that we had just half a day of school. My Abuelita Aura had retired as a cleaning woman in the city because the commute was too onerous. My abuelitas were getting older and would not question me if I told them I had half a day. I had been intimate with girls over the years but I had never made love to a woman. I had a lot of practice kissing and experience with foreplay. I had seen a few porno movies as there was a theater in my old neighborhood that played porno movies. I would go with some of the neighborhood kids, and they would let us in even though we were kids. I had porn magazines that I bought at the local convenience store, where they also sold me wine coolers even though I was underage. There were a few occasions when I would buy explicit XXX magazines and the store clerk would give me funny looks or adults would give me dirty looks. I remember once the store clerk told me as I was paying for a magazine, "You are going to like this one; it's going to take you to the next dimension." There was an elderly woman that could have been someone's grandmother waiting in line behind me and she looked like she was ready to have a heart attack. After that day I stopped buying porn and I stopped going to that store.

For my school-skipping, lovemaking date with Linda, I wore my favorite outfit: a white Polo dress shirt, light-colored Levis jeans and a pair of penny loafers. I took an extra-long shower that morning and even blow-dried my hair with my mom's dryer. I applied extra deodorant and wore the sexiest bikini underwear in my collection. I have no idea why, but for Christmas, my abuelitas bought me sexy bikini underwear, one tiger-striped and the other leopard-spotted. They were probably on sale at some department store and my abuelitas probably didn't know what type of underwear they were buying for me. I had saved up some money and bought Polo cologne, which I splashed on my palms and all over my face and chest. Later, Linda would tell me to cool it with all the cologne. Over the years, I had been indulging in so much cologne on special occasions that my nose must have become desensitized. I was a workout warrior back then and I had rock-hard abs and a streamlined body, so I looked good in my bikini underwear. Thanks, Abuelita! I met Linda at a diner near her house, and we had breakfast before our big day. She wore a black, form-fitting mini skirt and a pretty white ruffled blouse with cute white sandals. She looked lovely and she smelled great. I was ready to jump over the table and attack her at the diner. We had a few hours to kill to make it look good before we got to my house, but after a while we couldn't wait any longer and we got to my house before noon. My Abuelita Aura asked what we were doing home so early, and I said we had half a day of school. She looked at me like she knew I was up to something, but she let us in and went downstairs to her basement apartment. My parents and my sister had rooms upstairs and my Abuelita Aura and Abuelita Hortencia lived in the basement. My Abuelita Hortencia kept my room immaculate, and it was pristine that day.

    I took Linda to my room. I had to act cool because I wanted her first time to be special. I had bought a special candle and when we walked into my room, I lit the rose-scented candle and put a mix tape of romantic songs in my radio/cassette player. I walked her to my bed and began to gently kiss her neck. We kissed for what seemed like hours. At first, we started light and sweet and then it became heavy and frantic. We were caressing and enjoying each other's bodies and then she gently took off her blouse. She then took down her miniskirt and she was in her bra and panties. I quickly took off my clothes and I was suddenly in my tiger stripe bikini underwear. I could tell she liked my body because she had that look on her face like she was panting and gasping for air. I was pleasantly surprised because she had a nice body, and I was always used to seeing her in baggy sporty clothes. I took off her bra slowly. At that moment it was not a romantic move, I just had never taken a woman's bra off and I wanted to make sure I did it right. I found the clasp quickly and it came right off. I was relieved and happy – so far so good. I had to hold back from screaming, "Yes! Yes! I did it!"

    When I saw her breasts for the first time, I became very excited and rock-hard. She had really nice breasts, which I had never truly noticed because they were always hidden underneath her baggy clothes. She was a D cup, and I never even knew. I kissed her neck and kissed her all over her body. I was trying to get her excited and show her that I knew what I was doing. I sucked on her nipples, caressed her body and massaged her from head to toe. I slowly removed her panties, and I could see that they were all wet. I could smell her lovemaking scent. It was a strong and sweet smell. I softly blew into her ear and pressed her naked body against mine. She started moaning and groaning "Edwin, please, I want it."

It was time and I slowly pulled her closer to me. She had light-colored pubic hair that was glistening because she was so wet. I never lost my cool and kept trying to be smooth. I refused to just stick it in and have an orgasm in two seconds the way you hear about young guys having sex for the first time.

Years earlier, my Tía Diana and her new middle-aged husband Elmer had given me good advice even though I had not asked for it or wanted it, especially from them. They told me that women don't want it to be over so quickly, and they want to enjoy the lovemaking. Elmer told me to use mind techniques to calm myself down and avoid coming too fast. He told me to think about things that would turn me off while I am stroking. Linda and I fell to the bed, and she spread her legs. I positioned myself on top of her and tried to put my penis inside her vagina. This was the part where no matter how many times you see it you cannot know exactly where the opening is. I fumbled a little and Debbie grabbed my manhood and guided it in. I don't know if that gave it away, but I don't think she cared because she looked like she was hyperventilating and ready to pass out. Once my manhood was in, I could hear a squishing sound; Debbie was very wet. I felt like I was putting my penis into warm rice pudding or a warm apple pie. I was so excited, and it felt so good that I felt like I wanted to explode immediately. I kept my cool and thought about my abuelita washing dishes which sounds sick, but it was the least sexual thing I could think about. We continued making love for some time. I lost track of the time, but I know that I saw her shake and shiver a few times. I did not know back then when or how women had orgasms. Then I could no longer hold back anymore, and I had to pull out violently as I was not wearing a condom and I was not ready to get anyone pregnant, so I came on the side of my bed. Linda and I were definitely going to be doing that a lot more!

    Linda and I started having more and more half days. I would get truancy letters sent home from school and I would take them out of the mailbox and throw them in the trash. The worst possible thing that could have happened at that time, happened. My abuelitas went to Colombia to visit family for two months. By then, my little sister was eight years old, and she was mature for her age. She took a school bus to and from school every day. When my abuelitas left for Colombia, I started bringing Linda to the house every day. It's funny that before my Abuelita Aura left, she told me to stop bringing that girl over all the time and skipping school. She said I was like a little boy with a new toy at Christmas. She said in Spanish, "*le da, le da, y le da*," meaning I kept playing with that new toy over and over again. Linda and I were having sex every day, like newlyweds. We started getting creative in our lovemaking. I would rub her down and massage her with baby oil and lotions. We experimented with different positions. I even put chocolate syrup, whipped cream, ice cream and fruit all over her body and ate it while making love to her. I was having fun, but I knew that I was ruining my life at the same time.

    I was attending one of the most prestigious high schools in

the country and I was flushing my education down the toilet. It wasn't just Linda or the sex, it was the commute, my dislike for my new teachers, my teenage anger toward my father and the world, and my overall unhappiness. I just felt like my life was spiraling out of control. I would go back to school from time to time to see my old friends and hang out in the cafeteria. I would take random exams from time to time in the hopes that some of my teachers would pass me based on my test grades. I even joined the handball team that spring of '86. I could not believe that the New York City Public School Athletic League recognized handball as a sport. Our handball coach was also the swimming coach, and he knew nothing about handball. I'm sure he took the job just to make some extra money. His advice was, "Keep hitting the ball hard and keep winning." I was one of the best players on the team along with another Latino student, Harry, from Sunset Park in Brooklyn. Harry and I would tell him, "Don't worry, coach, we've got this!" I loved playing handball and it felt good being part of a team again. We played against other Brooklyn Schools and won all of our matches. We were good and we even won our division and qualified for the playoffs with the chance to become New York City champions. I had won track races before, but never any championships. Unfortunately, the second marking period grades came out and I was ruled academically ineligible, as I was failing multiple classes because of my truancy. In an embarrassing turn of events, Harry was also declared academically ineligible, and the team had to withdraw from playoff contention. Not a proud day for the Latino community at Tech. It would have been fun to lord it over our rival teams and boast that the Brooklyn Tech Engineers, considered nerds by the other players, kicked everyone's ass and won the city championship.

After getting ruled academically ineligible from the handball team and flunking most of my classes, I felt like I had hit rock bottom. My father saw my report card and yelled and screamed at me for hours. He did not hit me anymore, but I felt angry and ashamed. He said a lot of hurtful things out of anger, including that I would amount to nothing and that I was a bum. No longer the prodigy, I was now a disappointment in his eyes. My mother comforted me afterward and we spoke for hours. I could see the shame in her eyes, which hurt more than anything my dad could ever do to me. That look on my mother's face hit me hard and I cried hysterically in her arms. After that, I continued to see Linda, but we were drifting apart. We were just kids and, honestly, our relationship was only sustained by sex. I was young and dumb but that's just the way it was, I can't take any of it back.

    Linda and I did not have a lot in common. One Saturday night that year my parents had a big party at the house. It was the usual drinking and dancing Latino house party, and all our family and friends were invited. In our new house, the parties took place in the basement. One family, old Colombian friends of ours, came all the way from New Jersey that night. I used to hang out with their daughter Thalia whenever we all got together at the beaches, lakes, and rivers back in the day, but I had not seen her in a couple of years. Thalia was my age and had filled out nicely. I had never seen her with makeup on; she was wearing a form-fitting dress and looked good, having blossomed into womanhood. While all the adults were at the party in the basement, Thalia and I hung out in my room. She started kissing my neck and I told her to stop because I had a girlfriend. She didn't care and told me that she had a boyfriend, but that he was religious and wouldn't touch her and she was horny. That was good enough for me, she didn't have to twist my arm, and we fooled around that night. Thalia left me with a parting gift, a virus: infectious mononucleosis. I found out because I began to feel a sharp pain in my left side and felt extremely weak. My parents thought I was faking it because I did not want to go to school. When I went to see the doctor, he suspected that I had infectious mononucleosis. The blood tests came back positive for mono. The doctor told me that my spleen was enlarged and that it could burst, so I was placed on bed rest for four to six weeks. We had to call Thalia's family and they confirmed that their daughter had infectious mononucleosis and she had given it to me. Her family was furious as they had become deeply religious and the whole affair was scandalous. I never saw Thalia or her family again, even though my family was invited to Thalia's wedding years later. We didn't go, but I wonder if she married that religious boyfriend that she was dating when we hooked up. I had cheated on my girlfriend, and I knew that what we thought was a magical relationship was not going to last. My parents had kept harassing me about not having a girlfriend for years and even questioned whether I was gay. Not only was I not gay, it turned out that I was now a Latino lover. When I had to tell Linda that I contracted infectious mononucleosis from another girl, I felt like a Latino Loser!

I just could not lie to Linda, and when she cried hysterically, I felt very guilty. She finally stopped sobbing, but then she became furious with me for a while, until ultimately, she forgave me. I asked her to get tested for the virus, but she refused. She must have had a strong immune system because she never got sick, even though she kept spending time with me and kissing me. I told her to stay away for a while so I could recover. My dad told me to keep her away because I would not be able to resist the temptation of her incredible, hot body. Yes, that was very good advice, but creepy coming from my dad! After a few weeks Linda came to my house while my parents were out. My dad was right – we had sex. Linda told me to lie in bed and she would do all the work so I wouldn't exert myself. I think my spleen was still enlarged because I felt pain in my left side. Unfortunately, I was not fully recovered yet and while she was on top of me naked, I passed out. When I regained consciousness, I saw her dressed and crying over my lifeless body. I have no idea how long I was blacked out. Poor Linda thought she had killed me; she was hysterical and never told me how long I was unconscious. To this day, I have no idea how much time I lost, it could have been a few minutes or a few hours. Linda probably should have called 911, but I am sure she was too scared and nervous. Even so, I am glad she didn't just take off and leave me naked on my bed, and then my mother would have found me like that. Little did I know that something like that would actually occur, my mom would see me naked in my bed with my girlfriend.

Linda didn't come back until a few weeks later when the doctor gave me medical clearance to resume physical activity, including sports and presumably sex. As soon as I was cleared, Linda came over to my house on a Saturday morning while my parents and my eight-year-old sister Valeria were gone. When I let Linda into my room there was no small talk, we just fast-forwarded to the sex like a prisoner and his girlfriend after he is released from prison. I was feeling better, although still a little weak, but she just attacked me. I was a teenager, and my hormones were out of control. We were having sex and before I could climax, I saw that my bedroom door was being opened and I panicked and kept going instead of stopping immediately. What was I thinking! It was my mother and I screamed, "Ma, close the door!" She was in shock and just stood there frozen in time with her mouth open and a blank stare on her face. I was so embarrassed that I couldn't move, and she finally closed the door.

I loved my mother, and we were very close. However, she felt uncomfortable talking about sex, at least to me. Nobody gave me the birds and the bees talk, I just sort of figured it out on my own. My mother had happened upon some porn magazines that I had hidden in one of my drawers. They were European erotica magazines and were as hardcore as they come. She told me that they were disgusting and that I should never do those revolting things that were in the magazine. How could I possibly respond to that request?

Now I had to explain, "Look, Ma, I am doing those disgusting things with my girlfriend." My mother was liberal and open-minded, but she was not comfortable discussing sexuality with me. She claimed to be a virgin when she was married, but I know that she did have sex with my father before she was married because she was three months pregnant during her wedding ceremony. Personally, I would prefer that my wife-to-be would be a virgin for selfish reasons but honestly, I would never want my future wife to ever wonder what it would be like to be with another man because she had never been with anyone else. My future wife told me that my mother once told her that she had regrets because she had never been with another man and wondered what it would be like. In regard to catching her son having sex in his room with his girlfriend, that was the end of any privacy I would ever have in my room with any girl ever, until the day that I was married. Even a few days before my wedding, my mom had me sleep in the basement while my bride-to-be slept in my room.

My abuelitas came back from Colombia with my Tía

Carmen at the end of the summer of '86. My Tía Carmen came to the United States to start a new life for herself when she was only nineteen years old. Between my abuelitas, my Tía Carmen, my impressionable eight-year-old sister Valeria, and my traumatized mom, my Casanova days at the house were over. An alarm would sound if I ever brought a girl to the house, as if a bank were being robbed and one of the tellers activated an ear-piercing alarm. My Abuelito Antonio (my mom's father) left my Abuelita Aura (my mom's mother) for a younger woman, Margarita. To make matters even more interesting, my Abuelito Antonio never married my Abuelita Aura. He did marry Margarita and they had three children, including my Tía Carmen. Now Carmen would be living in the basement of my house with my Abuelita Aura. The living arrangement can only be described as scandalous, but this kind of situation frequently happens in Latino households. My mother loved her dad and her (half) sister Carmen, which is why she came to stay with us. Poor Carmen had to experience all my teenage drama, and to this day she still teases me about my adolescent years.

At that time my great-grandmother, Abuelita Hortencia, was in her 80s and becoming senile. I was raised by my great-grandmother, and I loved her more than anything in the world. When I was a little boy, she would shoplift candy and toys for me. I saw her get caught once at a Woolworth's retail store in the old neighborhood, and she put on the little old lady crying show. The security guard and the store manager were deceived by the tears and let her go. As we walked out of the store, she stopped crying and gave me a wink and a smile. I was impressed by her performance and loved her even more if that was possible. My Abuelita Hortencia outlived two husbands in Colombia. When I was a child, my mom told me that they both abused her, and they both ended up dying mysteriously. Her first husband Eduardo had his throat slashed when he was out in the fields, working as a day laborer. Nobody was ever caught, and his death was attributed to the guerrillas during a time of political turmoil. Her second husband, Abelardo, mysteriously died of poisoning. The authorities never identified a suspect, and the murder is still unsolved. Was it foul play, was my Abuelita Hortencia the original black widow, or was it just karma? I believe it was the original WOKE movement – if you violate or abuse me, I will put you to sleep! My family has many secrets that went to the grave with our deceased relatives, so I will never know for sure. That's why Latinos love the telenovelas/soap operas because life imitates art and art imitates life. When I was a kid in the old neighborhood, in the summer I would play out in the streets all day and come home to a buffet: rice and beans, carne asada, sancocho, tostones and ensalada. After dinner, my Abuelita Hortencia would serve me dessert, usually homemade rice pudding with raisins and cinnamon. It would always be fresh and hot and melt in your mouth. I was eating restaurant-quality food on a daily basis as a kid. I never had leftovers until after I was married.

 When my Abuelita Hortencia found out that I was prohibited from having girls in my room, she created a little love nest in my garage. She cleaned a little section in the back, laid down fresh blankets and a pillow, and placed some plants, candles, and a small, battery-operated radio around the space. She meant well, but no self-respecting girl was going to have sex with me in a nasty garage with a cold concrete floor, decaying wood and clutter including tires, tools, and the sweet aroma of gasoline smells. It was a nice gesture, but I never used that little love nest.

CHAPTER 11

My relationship with Linda was already on life support and, predictably, we broke up. With a few exceptions, high school sweethearts eventually break up or get married and then divorced. As a teenager, you are only starting to get to know yourself. People hook up for the wrong reasons and think they are in love. Another heartbreaking pill that I had to swallow was that I fell behind in my studies at Tech, so much so that I could not catch up and I would not be able to graduate with my class. I made the decision to transfer to my zoned school, Bayside High School. Mark Tatum, the deputy commissioner of the National Basketball Association, was part of my class at Brooklyn Tech. Many future CEOs, executives and progressive, successful people who I was proud to call my friends graduated from Brooklyn Technical High School in 1987. My buddy Yusef d up working for NASA as an engineer. The list goes on and on, but I would not be one of those graduates. Despite all the years of commuting, struggling, working hard, and studying late and all the friends that I made, I would never be able to call myself a Brooklyn Tech graduate. I missed my senior prom, my graduation and finishing my studies at one of the most storied high schools in the country. I don't blame anyone but myself; I still consider it to be one of my biggest regrets in life.

James, one of the football players on my former team, continued to be a good friend even after I left Tech. He knew that I was down about transferring schools and breaking up with

Linda, so he asked me to hang out with him to help me take my mind off things. He told me to meet him at the Times Square Train Station near the N Train stop. It happened to be my birthday, and I had no clue what was in store for me that night! James was running late, which is normal for most Latinos. In the late 80s it was still cool to smoke, and I used to smoke cigarettes occasionally. So, I pulled out a cigarette and lit it. Unfortunately, I was still at the train station behind the turnstiles, where James had asked me to meet him because the Times Square Station is massive with a great deal of foot traffic. Two police officers approached me while I was smoking. I had absolutely no clue that it was illegal to smoke inside a train station. I just continued to puff away, and they must have thought I was being defiant. When one of the officers slapped the cigarette out of my mouth, I was shocked and upset. Then they began to interrogate me, asking if I had any drugs or if I was selling drugs. They frisked me and asked me if I had any weapons on me. I felt violated and embarrassed because many people at this point were looking at me as if I were a lowlife criminal. We were putting on a show for the tourists, but I was not a willing participant. One of the officers asked me if I had a criminal record and when I said no the other officer said: "Yeah right, stop lying!" They radioed in my pedigree information to see if I had any outstanding warrants. I was angry because I was being tried and convicted for being a suspicious-looking young Latino. After harassing me for nearly half an hour, those officers gave me a ticket for smoking on the train and told me that I was lucky that they did not take me to the police station and lock me in a cell. They wanted me to be thankful! I refused to give them the satisfaction and after they gave me the ticket one of the officers told me, "I will be seeing you soon and maybe if we're lucky, even tonight. Next time we see you were going to cuff you, kick your ass and lock you up!"

I wanted to tell them, "Seriously, get a life and go after the real bad guys."

A few years later I was at a nightclub in Greenwich Village in New York City, hanging out with some friends. There was a band playing and the place was packed. Unfortunately, the bar only had one unisex restroom and there was a line out the door to use the facilities. I had been drinking half the night and I had to pee very badly! I flashed back to when I was a little kid in first grade and I desperately needed to go to the bathroom, but the teacher refused to let me go, so when I couldn't hold it anymore, I peed myself. Shaking that image out of my head, I ran out of the bar in search of an alley or a quiet place where I could pee. Ah ha! I saw some steps leading down to a small apartment on McDougal Street. I ran down those steps and peed violently on someone's apartment door. It felt so good that I was moaning and groaning; it must have sounded like I was having sex. My pee seemed to stream freely for minutes and then suddenly I felt a tap on my shoulder from behind me. I had been more worried about someone opening the door in front of me. It was a police officer, who said: "Hey buddy, I hope you're enjoying yourself." He was nice about it and let me finish before he gave me a ticket. It was my second violation, which is a criminal offense but not a crime. A crime is a misdemeanor or felony and thank God I never had any of those. Years later, when I passed the bar exam and needed to be admitted as an attorney, I had to pass an interview with the Character and Fitness committee. In law school, we were all warned to divulge all information regardless of whether we wanted to or not. The Character and Fitness committee could reject your application if information that you failed to disclose came to light. The interview would take place at the office of the famous attorney Harry Dicker of Wilson, Elser, Moskowitz and Dicker, a prominent law firm. Harry Dicker was an imposing man with silver hair and bushy eyebrows; sitting majestically in his raised mahogany chair, he examined my application folder, looked down at me and questioned me about smoking on the train and peeing in the street. I was deeply embarrassed and wanted to hide under his desk. What could I say, other than I was young and dumb, and youth is wasted on the young!

Back at the train station, James showed up an hour late and with a big smile on his face he told me that he was sorry and that he would make it up to me. I was beyond angry as I told him what happened with the cops, and he did not believe me. James dad was of Puerto Rican descent and his mom was Irish. He did not speak Spanish and he looked like a white boy. His last name was Cruz, but it might as well have been McGillicuddy. He was six foot two, fair-skinned and had sandy blond hair and green eyes. I laughed when I brought him to the house one day and my Tía Carmen fell in lust with him. He could not comprehend what had happened to me with the police. I lived in New York my whole life and was commuting to Brooklyn for high school, but I had never been to Times Square. James told me that he knew his way around and I should follow him. I had just turned seventeen, and I was wondering what my birthday surprise would be. First, we walked about a block from the train station where I had been interrogated and went to a place called Peep World. It was like an arcade where you turn in your money for tokens. I didn't know what to expect, but obviously James had been there before because he knew the drill. After we bought our tokens, we went into private booths and a small window opened after we inserted our tokens. Then I saw many naked women dancing on a stage that was surrounded by multiple windows where customers would have a view of the stage. The dancers were mostly white, Black, and Latino and I was surprised at how pretty and attractive some of these women were. I was shocked that they would subject themselves to this. One token was only a dollar, so how much money could these girls be making? Perhaps these girls had drug addictions or were forced to work there by pimps or mobsters. Today you hear about foreign women who come to this country with promises of good jobs and citizenship opportunities and are forced to work as strippers or prostitutes. At the time I had no idea about this seedy part of New York City. Back then the strip club explosion was just beginning.

    I sat there gawking for a while and then a pretty, light-skinned Black girl came up to the window and asked me to touch her. I swear she looked a lot like Vanity, a famous singer and actress from the '80s! What? Yes, of course. I caressed her breasts and her nipples. It was November and it was chilly outside. I vividly remember the dancer saying: "Baby, your hands are cold, let me warm them up." She took my hands and put them between her legs so they would warm up. I started tipping her with dollar bills and after a few minutes the window would close, and I would have to put another token in the slot so the window would stay open. It was like playing video games with benefits. If I had seen or met that girl in a bar or a club, I would have bought her a drink or asked for her phone number. That night for a couple of bucks we cut to the chase, except without having sex. I wondered how on earth James found this place. We were only seventeen years old. As much fun as I was having, I was running out of tokens, and it was time to go. When I exited the booth, I started paying close attention to my surroundings. That place was disgusting. I could hear moans and groans coming from all the booths, and you could tell that men were masturbating inside those booths. There were also other booths that did not have live girls but showed porno movies. This place was like a Dave and Busters or an arcade for degenerates. I saw a janitor running around with a mop from booth to booth. I don't know how much they paid that poor dude but it could not be enough. I once had a part-time job at a Waldbaum's supermarket where they would page me to clean up spills in the aisles. I would hear on the intercom, "Edwin, we have a spill in aisle six," for example. A little boy would break a peanut butter jar, or a senior citizen would drop a jar of spaghetti sauce because they couldn't grip it properly due to arthritis in their hands. I thought that supermarket job was demeaning, and I quit. This Peep World clean up duty, however, took it to another level. Johnny, we have a spill in booths 6, 7, 8, 9, 10, etc. That poor guy probably had nightmares when he got home after a shift.

I finally saw James come out of his booth, looking flushed and sweaty. I couldn't believe it! I was not going to shake his hand for the rest of the night. I told him, "Let's get the hell out of here!"

He said, "Relax, I've got a better place we can go to next."

We walked along Eighth Avenue for a few blocks, from 42nd to 49th Street and it seemed like an obstacle course full of pimps, prostitutes, hustlers, thieves, homeless people, degenerates, and drug dealers. If you remember the old Mel Gibson post-apocalyptic *Mad Max* movies or the popular zombie series *The Walking Dead* that's what Times Square looked like in the late 80s. We walked only seven blocks, but it felt like we were approached by hundreds of people: "Yo, you lookin' to get laid? You wanna get high? How about a blow job? Yo, you lookin' to buy some jewelry?"

When we finally arrived at the club, I had to check my back pocket to make sure that my wallet was still there.

There was a line to get in, but James knew the guy at the front door, and he let us right in. This was not Studio 54 or some glamorous club, it was a sex club. We found seats and when the show started, an attractive Black woman stripped naked on a stage and began to touch herself and moan and groan. I was not totally disgusted, even somewhat turned on, but when the audience members started taking out their ding dongs and jerking off, that was too much. I wanted to throw up. Then some random guy who I thought was an usher walked onto the stage and began having sex with the dancer. He was not an attractive man and I felt that she deserved better. I could not believe that this subculture existed in New York. To put all this into context, many of the places we visited or walked past that night are tourist attractions in 2021. Times Square has been transformed for the better and is now a popular and famous tourist attraction. Today tourists can see cartoon characters and Muppets like Elmo or the Cookie Monster in their costumes, asking for tips and volunteering to take pictures. I saw a lot of prostitutes, pimps, drug dealers, hustlers, and all types of strange-looking characters that night when I was there. Today the entire Times Square area is filled with Disney stores, Disney-themed restaurants, and family-friendly attractions. All the restaurants and theaters in the Times Square area are family friendly. Back then it was a cesspool, and no family would be caught dead in that area after hours. Today you have the Hard Rock Café, attractions like the National Geographic Ocean Odyssey, Madame Tussauds wax museum and Marvel superhero-themed adventures for kids and adults. Change is not always good, but in this case it definitely was.

My birthday adventure with James continued because he talked me into walking to the Port Authority bus terminal in Times Square to look for girls. The idea was to meet girls that were coming from all parts of the country to pursue their hopes and dreams of becoming an actress or model, singer, or entertainer. Buses from all over the country would come to the Port Authority in New York City with beautiful women full of hopes and dreams of making it in the Big Apple. When we got to the Port Authority, all I saw were homeless people sleeping on benches and in the waiting areas, and lowlifes walking around looking to prey on out-of-towners. Sadly, I did not see any pretty women from small-town USA, it was more like strung-out women from NYC. I got tired of being harassed by panhandlers and bums, and I could not take the smells anymore, so I told James, "Let's get out of here!" I was beginning to suspect that James was addicted to porn and sex.

    He told me that he did not want to go home until he got laid. Then he started harassing me and asked me, "What about your old neighborhood – are there any spots that we could go to?"

    When I lived in the old neighborhood, everyone knew there were places where you could get laid, on or near 90th Street and Roosevelt Avenue. Nonetheless, I yelled at him, "Seriously, James, I haven't been there in years, and I don't need to pay to get laid!"

    He insisted and kept harassing me like a petulant child and told me, "Let's go, I got you covered." He was very persistent and after all, I had not been to the old neighborhood in years, so I gave in. The 7 train stop, which would take us to the 90th Street stop where we needed to go, was right there in Times Square. In New York City all the main train lines begin and end at Times Square. It always baffled me why it took so long to clean up the

Times Square area. It never made sense to me that the biggest, brightest city in the world was not safe for tourists. Perhaps the Mob and the underworld had political influence back then, with lobbyists that worked on behalf of their salacious interests. In my opinion, bribing some congressman or local politicians and police chiefs, captains, officers, and police personnel to maintain the status quo would never be sustainable. Times Square today generates billions of dollars in tourism and stimulates the New York City economy much more than any bribes or underworld counterculture ever could.

We took the 7 train to the 90th Street stop in Jackson Heights. It was after midnight when we stepped off the train, and it looked like Mardi Gras was in full swing on 90th Street and Roosevelt Avenue. I didn't recognize my old neighborhood. We heard gunshots, police and firetruck sirens, people screaming and loud music. I felt like we were in the Wild West. My old neighborhood was always dangerous and loud when I lived there, but not like this. James suggested, "Let's get some booze before we look for the women."

I was starting to wonder if this was my birthday celebration or was, he just using me? Less than a block away from the train station we found a bodega that sold us beer even though we were underage. We weren't even asked how old we were or for ID. We bought a couple of 40-ounce bottles of Old English Malt Liquor and drank them on our way to the brothel.

I had an idea about where it was located, from stories that I had heard back in the day. However, as we were drinking and hanging out in the street by Roosevelt Avenue, it became very obvious because there were a lot of men walking toward a house a few blocks away. The brothel was located a few blocks from the train station in a block that had residential houses. I am sure that many of those houses were drug fronts or stash houses for Colombian Cartels and God only knows what else; June and Ward Cleaver or Mike and Carol Brady were not living next door. We approached the house and rang the doorbell. Some scary-looking Latino dude, who did not have a neck and looked like he killed people for fun, opened the door.

"*Qué quieren?*" (What do you want?)

"*Estamos buscando mujeres.*" (We're looking for women.)

He let us in, and we walked up a flight of stairs to a waiting area. I felt like I was in a hospital waiting room; a lot of men were sitting there, waiting for their turn. James and I definitely looked out of place because everyone was older and ethnic looking. I didn't want to be involved, but James told me that he would pay and did not want to do it alone. I was used to being with young girls without having to pay to get laid, but he talked me into it.

The weird part was that we did not get to choose the girls. There was a manager of sorts who would escort whoever was next into one of the many bedrooms. James was picked after a few minutes and escorted into a room. He gave me twenty bucks before he left as he promised to pay for my woman. I was next and I was escorted into a room. My woman was an older Colombian woman who looked like she could have been one of my mother's friends. The smell was overwhelming. These hapless women were having sex with disgusting, sweaty, unhygienic men for hours on end. I was always sensitive to smells and I began to gag immediately. My lady was pretty, but she was older, and you could tell that her best years were behind her. We spoke for a while, and I tried to explain that my friend dragged me to this place. I volunteered to pay her and told her that I did not want to hurt her feelings. She was not having it and told me that I was cute, and she wanted to be with me. She took off my clothes and I did not resist, so as not to hurt her feelings. She began to suck my manhood, but I just could not get over the smell. She grabbed my hands and put them on her breasts and down her legs and body. I just could not get it up no matter how hard she tried. I could kill James – I did not want to do this!

I apologized and, after a while, she stopped trying. She said that I probably did too much cocaine or drank too much and that's why I couldn't get it up. I told her that she was probably right because I did not want to be rude. It was all amicable and we kissed goodbye with a little peck on the lips. When I sat back down in the waiting room, I did not see James. I was wondering if he did something to get himself killed. After what seemed like forever, he came out. He had that flushed look on his face again and he was sweating. This huge Amazon-like Colombian woman with giant breasts came out behind him yelling "Tip, Tip" with a heavy Spanish accent. I went up to him and asked him, " James, what the hell is going on?" He said that he did not want to give her a tip because he paid her a fair price. I could see the manager make a phone call and scary-looking dudes appeared. I had to apologize, and I gave that woman a tip out of my own pocket. That was the first and last time I would ever go to a brothel.

I was upset with James and I told him how to get home from Queens to Brooklyn. It was the same commute I had taken to go to high school for years. The 7 Train to Queens Plaza and then the N Train to Brooklyn. It was late and I was exhausted. I forgot where I was and when my train arrived, I sat down in the subway car and immediately fell asleep. You should never lose track of where you are in Jackson Heights, especially in those days. When I arrived at the last stop, I was woken up by the train conductor. It was late at night and the train was going to the yard. When I looked down, I felt a breeze near my pants pocket area because I had a hole where my right pocket was. I had transferred my wallet to my front pants pocket at the end of the night because I did not want anyone to pick my back pocket. While I was passed out someone had carefully cut my pants pocket. I could not believe it. Whoever cut my pants pocket could have done anything to me, and that freaked me out. I got off the train and went to the bus stop to take the Q12 bus home. When I looked at the schedule, I saw that the buses stopped running at a certain hour and I had two hours to kill. Could this night, now morning get any worse? I walked into a nearby diner and asked to use the bathroom. The waitress looked at my pants and asked me what happened to me. After I told her the story, she felt bad for me and gave me breakfast on the house because I obviously didn't have any money.

When the bus finally came, I tried to get on and the bus driver would not let me on without paying my fare. When I tried to tell him why I had no money he looked at me skeptically. I am sure he heard the same stories and excuses all the time. Finally, I showed him the hole in my pants, and he knew I could not be making this story up, so he let me on. God bless that bus driver! When I finally arrived at my stop and stumbled home, it was early morning. I walked into the house and my family was having breakfast. I had no clue what my father was going to do to me; I was older now, but he was always strict. He just said: "What are you, an owl?" and kept eating. I was so relieved, and I went to my room and passed out. After I met my future wife, she would forbid me to be friends with James. That may have been wise on her part.

I was only seventeen years old, and I felt like my life was spiraling out of control. My dad was barely talking to me, and he was always arguing with my mother. My antics were not helping the situation. He sent my poor sister to Catholic school because of me. My dad cut me off and stopped giving me money to hang out or buy clothes. My friend Elvin got me a part-time job at a neighborhood White Castle that was close to my new high school, which was convenient. Half of the employees were older immigrants, and the other half were young teenagers like me. One of the older workers told me that I should tell girls that I work at the French restaurant Le Château Blanc, or a fancy restaurant called the WC Steakhouse, whose initials stand for White Castle. I didn't need to lie about where I worked, because I felt like a fox in a hen house. There were many pretty young girls working at that White Castle, and I dated all of them. One afternoon, Ruth, who was one of the managers and was in her twenties, started coming on to me. At first, I felt uncomfortable because she was older, but she looked good in that uniform. She used to work out and it showed because she liked to wear her uniform extra tight. She had big breasts, a small waist and a nice butt, and she was cute in her own way, but I wouldn't call her beautiful. The problem was that Ruth was engaged. It was hard to hold her off because she was so aggressive in her pursuit. She would order me to go to the basement to perform tasks and then she would follow me and basically attack me, but I didn't try very hard to fight her off. We started seeing each other but I made it clear I just wanted to have fun and that she should not even think about leaving her fiancé. One night after work a bunch of us went to my backyard to hang out and have wine coolers. We were making a lot of noise and all of a sudden after we got liquored up, a bunch of us started fooling around. Ruth jumped on top of me in my backyard and told me that she wanted me right then and there. We were with other people, and I was not comfortable having sex in public like that, in an orgy setting.

Of course, my dad came out in his bathrobe and slippers when Ruth was on top of me. He yelled at me *"Este no es un hotel!"* (This is not a hotel!) He told us all to leave immediately; I am glad that he didn't grab me by my ear like when I was a kid. Once again, I thought back to those days when he worried that I was gay and harassed me about not having a girlfriend. Look, Dad, I am straight, and I have a lot of girlfriends. Ruth and I had to stop seeing each other because I could not take the guilt, as she was engaged, and she wanted more than I could give her. I think I was too young to be dealing with that type of relationship.

Instead of taking some time off from seeing women, the way I should have, I jumped right back on the horse. I was hanging out on Bell Boulevard in my new neighborhood near White Castle one night with my friends Elvin, Luis and Jerry. We saw a pretty blond girl walking out of the White Castle. She looked like Rebeca De Mornay, the actress that played the love interest in *Risky Business*, the cult movie classic with Tom Cruise. We all stared at her, and my knucklehead friends dared me to talk to her. I went up to her and started a conversation. I found out that her name was Emma. I think she was surprised because I was well-spoken and well-read. We talked for a while and then I asked for her phone number. She told me that she was engaged to be married. That was that and I wished her good luck.

One month later on a Saturday night in July, I was home watching a New York Yankee baseball game. My mom knocked on my bedroom door and told me that some people were looking for me. I was enjoying the game and pigging out on junk food. I thought it was my knucklehead friends Elvin and the crew, and I was prepared to tell them to get lost. That night I just wanted to relax and watch the game. My hair was a mess, and I was wearing old sweatpants and a T-shirt.

I went to the door, and I saw a couple that I knew from my part-time job at White Castle, Peter and Elizabeth. How did they know where I lived? Apparently, Emma had asked them about me and someone from work must have told them where I lived. After I opened the door, they told me that they had a surprise for me. Suddenly, Emma stepped out from behind them. I never expected to see her again. I froze and I couldn't breathe. This kind of stuff only happens in movies, when the girl of your dreams comes looking for you on a random Saturday night. Peter had a car and drove us to Long Beach that night. Emma and I talked for hours. She had broken up with her fiancé and told me that she could not stop thinking about me. She had graduated from high school a few years back and was trying to figure out what to do with herself. Her dad owned a glass company, and her mother was a lawyer, so her family had money. Emma told Elizabeth and Peter that night at the beach that we were going for a walk in the moonlight. I took that as code that she wanted to have sex with me. We went for a walk on the beach and proceeded to make love under the stars. It was romantic until the sand started to bother us, since we had no blankets or even towels. Emma told me later that she had wanted to go for just a walk, but she couldn't help herself. We connected immediately and we would date for the next two years.

After that first night, we were boyfriend and girlfriend. We spoke on the phone for hours every day and could not get enough of each other. She was very smart and interesting, and we had a lot in common: she, too, was rebelling against her parents and had underachieved in school. The first few weeks of our relationship was a whirlwind romance, and very early on, she told me she loved me. She wanted me to meet her parents, so I went to her house one evening to meet them. I dressed conservatively with jeans and a white dress shirt and penny loafers. I was now a high school graduate and was going to a competitive college in New York City. I was well-read and well-spoken, and I was in excellent shape as I worked out on a daily basis. I was falling for Emma and I was looking forward to impressing her parents. When we walked in, her parents looked at me like I was the hired help, or maybe like a Latino landscaper who cut their grass. In the two years that I dated Emma, I never had a real conversation with either of her parents, it was always small talk. They never even gave me a chance and I felt like I was always going to be a lowlife loser to them. Whenever I went to the house, the rule was that we had to go to the basement. I was never allowed on the main floor, or the second floor where the bedrooms were. I convinced Emma to go back to school and she began taking classes at the local community college. She was reconnecting with her parents because she was not hanging out at all hours of the night with her crazy friends. She began working at her dad's office as a part-time bookkeeper and was wearing normal clothes, not the outrageous outfits she used to wear when she was into the punk rock scene before she met me. Despite all these changes for the better, her family never saw the connection. The first year that we were dating, Emma invited me to her house for Thanksgiving. When I arrived, the whole extended family was sitting at the dining room table, joking and laughing and having a good time. Once I walked in, there was silence. Emma introduced me, but no one shook my hand or said a word to me. Nobody at the table even made eye contact with me. I sat down and ate as quickly as possible and left with Emma. Once I stepped away from the table, they all started laughing and joking again. You cannot make this stuff up! No one even attempted to be friendly to me. The final blow was when her younger brother

Colin met a nice Irish/Italian girl, and she started coming to the house. She was allowed on the main floor and was allowed in Colin's bedroom. Emma had asked me to marry her, and I said no because we were too young. I don't know how serious she was, but it was unrealistic. She loved me and wanted to marry me, but her parents never met my parents or had any interest in meeting my family. Our relationship was doomed from the beginning because I was Latino, and her family would never accept me. It was a tough pill to swallow.

Emma was into punk rock. A lot of her friends were spoiled rich kids, but they tried to live the punk rock lifestyle. They all had multiple piercings, mohawks, orange, purple and pink hair and wore outrageous outfits. When they were all together, they looked like they were going to a Halloween party. They liked to party, drink, smoke pot and do drugs. Whenever I hung out with them, I could fit into that aspect of the culture, but I never tried to dress like them. It seemed like they all lived in fancy houses and mansions. Someone's parents were always traveling to Europe or some other exotic place, so we could have all night parties at their houses.

On several occasions, I woke up with Emma in someone else's bed; I remember after one crazy party I woke up on someone's kitchen floor. Despite the fact that I dated Emma and I partied with her friends, they only tolerated me because of her. It had nothing to do with the way I dressed because some of the punk rock crew dressed normally and had mainstream jobs. Everyone in the group was white and privileged, and they never accepted me because I was Latino. When they talked behind my back and took shots at me, I only found out because Emma would tell me. I was stupid for putting up with that nonsense, but she always begged me to forgive them and told me that she loved me.

I was a young, fit, good-looking, well-read, Latino teenager who was going to college, and they all treated me like a lowlife despite being treated like outcasts themselves by society because of the way they looked and dressed. That never made any sense to me.

Before graduating from high school, I had spent a year rebelling against my father, arguing with him constantly, cutting classes and moving out for weeks to live with an older Latino friend, Rodrigo, who was a school custodian and had his own apartment. I finally finished high school at my zoned school, Bayside High. Because I was behind academically, I graduated mid-year in January 1988. There was no prom, no cap and gown, no ceremony and no pomp and circumstance. My "graduation event" took place in the principal's office with a few other students. I received a limp handshake and my diploma from the principal. My parents were not there and to be honest I was embarrassed, so I am glad they did not attend. The commencement speech consisted of the principal telling us to turn in our school IDs and make sure our lockers were empty. Later that night, Emma and I had sex in a park next to the school, which was my prom and graduation present. We both had a warped sense of humor.

When I met Emma, I was getting my act together. I graduated from high school with a New York State Regents diploma. I always tested well, but I was punished by my teachers with low grades for skipping classes. I took SAT prep classes, and my dad helped me pay for them. He was confused because he thought I had given up on school and had no chance to get into college. I did not bother with any of the college counselors at Bayside High School because they would only see a lowlife Latino who was struggling in school, and they would push me toward trade school. Despite my mediocre grade point average, I scored at an elite level on the SAT. I filled out my own college applications and was accepted to Baruch College, considered to be the best College in the CUNY (City University of New York) system. My first choice was St. John's University, and I was pleased to be accepted there, but it was expensive, and I did not qualify for financial aid. My dad offered to pay for Baruch and not St. John's, so the decision was easy. I would be the first person to go to college in my family.

Before I started college, my mother began to feel tired and lethargic all the time, plus she was getting rashes on her skin. My dad and my abuelitas would tell her that she'd be fine; the Latino way was just to pray, and it would go away. I was very concerned and told my mom that she should see a doctor. I did the research and found her a good doctor she could see, near her job in the city. Starting as a young child, I was in charge of everything related to medical care and life-changing events for the family, as well as filling out applications. I used to take days off when I was in elementary school to take my abuelitas to the social security office. If my abuelitas were sick, I would take them to the doctor's office. When my cousin was dying of AIDS, I would take him to his medical appointments because no one else could. When my little sister had to have procedures done or she needed to go to a clinic, I would take her when no one else was available.

I took a day off from school to go with my mom to see an oncologist, whose office was near her job. After examining her and taking a blood sample, the doctor told us not to be overly concerned until the blood work results came back. I could see the look in his eyes, and I knew that he was holding something back from us. I could not tell my mother what I felt, but I knew that the news would not be good. When the results came in, the doctor told us the bad news: my mother had cancer! She was diagnosed with mycosis fungoides, a rare blood cancer also known as Alibert-Bazin syndrome or cutaneous T-cell lymphoma. It happens when white blood cells called T-cells grow out of control and move from the blood into the skin. Because of my inquisitive nature, I asked him for the best- and worst-case scenarios. I don't know if that doctor was just a straight shooter or if he could see how much I loved my mother and that I would not leave his office without an answer, but he told me she had ten years to live, tops. It was hard for me to explain it to my mother. We were on Water Street in the financial district of New York City, within walking distance of the New York Stock Exchange, on a Monday morning with all the movers and shakers walking by us like speeding cars on a highway.

I explained it to her carefully, and then she asked, "I have cancer and the most that I will live is ten years?"

"Sí, Mami, I am so sorry for everything!"

We both broke down and cried, right there in the street, and I hugged her as tight as I have ever hugged anyone. I thought back to my rebellious teenage years and all the suffering I had caused her because of my growing pains. I wish I could take it all back and do it over again. If only God had told me, I would have done it differently. "I am so sorry, Mami, I love you so much, please no." I could not be strong for her at that moment, just comforting. I believed the doctor, and I would never lie to my mother ever again! Emma abandoned me at this time because she didn't know how to console or comfort me. Her family's feelings about me made it easy for her to end the relationship. In retrospect it was for the best because if we had married, sooner or later I would have been just another Latino who was divorced at a young age.

I have always been a realist, but my mom was an optimist.

After that initial jolt of reality, she made me promise not to tell the family what the doctor said because she wanted to explain it to everyone in her own way. I kept my promise. My poor sister was only ten years old and my abuelitas were getting old and would not understand. My father was working long hours and was starting to become afflicted with rheumatoid arthritis. My mom did not want the family to be upset. My mother became a vegetarian and changed her lifestyle; she was determined to beat her illness by using a holistic approach and I was rooting for her. With a heavy heart, I looked forward to making her proud as the first person in our family to go to college.

CHAPTER 12

Baruch College, often called the crown jewel of CUNY (City University of New York universities), was the place to be in the late 80s, when big business was thriving. The movie *Wall Street*, with Michael Douglas and Charlie Sheen, was a smash hit. The famous line, "Greed, for a lack of a better word, is good," became a mantra and everyone was looking to get rich. The great thing about Baruch College was that even though it was an elite business school, it was not expensive. For my first year at Baruch, the tuition was $650 a semester. Everyone that went to Baruch in the late 80s had hopes and dreams of becoming successful. For many inner-city minorities that excelled in high school, Baruch was a great opportunity to gain a higher education and keep up with the elite white students who were going to private universities and Ivy League schools that were unaffordable for most First-Generation Latinos or minorities in general. It's interesting that Jennifer Lopez went to Baruch at the same time that I went. Jennifer Lopez's debut album was called *On the 6* because that was the train she took to go to Baruch from her neighborhood, Castle Hill in the Bronx. She dropped out after her freshman year because she found better opportunities. (That's an understatement.) For the other Latinos who went to Baruch, it provided an opportunity to get out of the hood, make a better life for themselves and make their families proud.

At an early age, I already knew that I would go to college, but now it was happening. That long winding road included self-inflicted detours, rebellious distractions, and forks in the road, but I survived growing up Latino in New York City in the '70s and '80s. I was waiting for my registration materials like a kid on Christmas Eve, waiting to open his presents at midnight. (I should explain that Latinos don't wait until December 25th to open presents, it's always at midnight on the night before Christmas. There are no milk and cookies for Santa, but rather loud salsa and merengue music and a lot of delicious food. In a Latino household, if we leave anything for Santa, it will be a little nip to shake off the Christmas Eve hangover in the morning.) When that big, fat registration package arrived, I was so happy I ripped it open like a kid opening his presents at Christmas. The package contained a thick book that outlined all the courses that were available at Baruch. I was surprised at how many courses were offered. I read that book from front to back and I was excited because there were so many diverse and interesting classes that were being offered. Going to college was going to be fun. For freshmen, a few classes were required, such as business organization and a few basic core curriculum classes, but you could start taking electives and fun courses from the beginning and you did not have to declare a major until junior year.

    I was excited about registering for my first semester as a college man. I put on my favorite outfit: a white Polo dress shirt, khakis, and penny loafers. I was going to submit my schedule early and then hang out in the city for a while. I went for a jog that morning, then shaved and showered. I felt like I was on top of the world! When I arrived at the office of the registrar it looked like there were thousands of people waiting in line to get tickets for a concert. I worked hard on my schedule so I knew I would be fine but, just in case, I had my alternate schedule ready. I got in the line and between the thousands of people and the lack of air conditioning, I started sweating profusely. I felt like I was at the Department of Motor Vehicles. People were yelling, and some people were even crying; I had been accepted early, but those people must have been late acceptances or on the fence, and they were likely on the bottom of the totem pole. I started wondering if I was in the right line. I waited patiently in the sweltering heat and oppressive humidity of late August, with sweat rolling down my face and body. I started regretting not wearing a tank top, shorts, and flip-flops. After waiting for what seemed like hours, I finally handed in my proposed schedule. I was told that the scuba diving elective that I had chosen was in the course book but was never offered due to a lack of funding, and all the other classes in my proposed schedule were either closed or not being offered that term. Thank God I had an alternate schedule! When I submitted my alternate schedule, none of the classes were available. Many classes were already filled to capacity and the remaining classes would close quickly. After hours of waiting, I was told to get out of the line and prepare a new schedule. Now I understood why people were screaming and crying. I ended up preparing at least ten different schedules and having to wait in line and then being told to leave multiple times. By the time I was done, my schedule was a disaster, with classes in the morning and in the evening. What was I going to do between classes? I was not able to take one of my required courses. How in the world was I going to graduate in four years if many of the required classes were unavailable? I ended up having to take a music appreciation class that first semester because nothing else was available. The sun was high in the sky when I arrived for registration, but when I left it was dark out. Welcome to CUNY in the late eighties.

    Nevertheless, I couldn't wait to begin my first semester as a college man. Baruch was unique because it was a commuter school. There were no dorms, and most students took the NYC subway system to get to school. In a sense, the city of New York was our campus. The only problem with going to school in the city was that everything was expensive, and there were no affordable meal plans. The school had buildings on 26th street and Park Avenue South, 18th street near Union Square Park, and 23rd and 24th street in Gramercy Park. These were some of the richest neighborhoods in New York City and possibly in the country. Despite the inconvenience, I enjoyed going to Baruch because I saw a lot of students that looked like me. Unfortunately, Latino women far outnumbered Latino men when I was a student at Baruch. One reason there were fewer Latino men going to college was that there were too many pitfalls in New York City back in the late 80s. Cocaine was prevalent all over the city and the crack epidemic was still going strong. Celebrities, investment bankers, and people from all walks of life that were into the party and club scene were buying cocaine at a record pace. Clubs like the Tunnel, Limelight, Club Exit, Sound Factory and Red Zone, where everyone who was anyone partied, were flooded with drugs.

The influx of illegal drugs – heroin, then cocaine and, next, crack cocaine – changed street gangs from social groups to business enterprises. The enactment of the Rockefeller Drug Laws in 1973 in New York, with stiffer prison sentences for dealers, had a negative effect on Latino youths. Facing possible hard time in prison, drug dealers began to recruit minors to do much of their selling on the streets. Young Latino drug dealers were becoming wealthy from selling drugs. Why go to college to get a good job and make a decent salary upon graduation, when you could become rich at a young age without going to school?

Of course, there was no long-term future in the drug game. Instead of a pension plan or 401K plan, there was early death or long-term incarceration. I believe that many of these young Latino hustlers and drug dealers had the street smarts, and the skill sets to become stockbrokers, entrepreneurs, or legitimate businessmen if they just would have gone to school. Other young Latinos who were not going to jail or getting killed wanted to work as soon as possible and did not even think about going to college. The immigrant work ethic is admirable and worthy of being emulated, but for those that could go to school and find better opportunities, higher education was not considered a viable option due to family pressure and negative influences. Many older Latino men who have dead-end jobs and are struggling to support their families wish they could have gone to school when they had a chance. While you are living with your family, even with a single mother or grandparents, it's possible to work and go to school. Many young Latinos mistakenly believe that it is important to get out of their parents' home as soon as possible, and they are in a big hurry to become adults and get a full-time job. However, once you are on your own or having to support your own family, going to school becomes difficult. I am an attorney today and I don't see a lot of people that look like me in court and at work.

While I was attending Baruch College, I made friends with the president of the Latino Student Organization, LASO. Coincidentally, his name was Ed and he lived in Spanish Harlem and was Puerto Rican. We became friends and hung out at a few parties. While attending college, he was a drug dealer on the side, with rich private clients, according to what he told me. In our sophomore year, he dropped out of school because he was making too much money dealing drugs and could not keep up with the demand. I wished him luck, after trying to talk him out of it. Today he could be a wealthy entrepreneur, or perhaps dead or incarcerated and doing hard time. I never saw or heard from him again. I hope that he made enough money to get out of the game and is living a good life somewhere, but I am highly doubtful.

Baruch was known as a business school with an elite accounting program, and many people in the business world graduated from Baruch. Just in my inner circle, my Latina wife Sandy is an accountant, and my Latino neighbor and friend Eric is an executive at Nike, and they are both Baruch graduates. However, I quickly found out that I enjoyed my liberal arts classes much more than my business classes. I took Black studies, Latin American Studies, sociology, anthropology and Spanish literature courses and I was hooked. Some of the professors were successful, intelligent people of color that looked like me and I could aspire to be like them. I still consider professors Wilson, Howard, Villar and Quintian to be mentors and minority professors of color that I admire. I was introduced to the works of some of the greatest writers in history, such as Richard Wright's famous novels *Native Son* and *Black Boy*, as well as Cervantes' groundbreaking *Don Quijote de La Mancha*. I was actually able to read the book *Don Quijote* in the original Spanish and it was challenging but fulfilling. I read books by Gabriel García Márquez, who is considered to be one of the greatest writers of all time and not only did he look like me, but he was from Colombia. At one of my family get-togethers, I met someone that knew him in Colombia. I felt so proud to have read his work and I never would have thought about reading any of his books, including *Cien Años de Soledad*, until I was informed about him by my Latin American studies professor. I was introduced to the works of Maya Angelou, Piri Thomas and so many other great writers of color by my professors at Baruch. I felt proud to be Latino and I enjoyed reading all these iconic books from writers that looked like me or who grew up like me, writers of color that made their marks on the world.

Baruch had a strong liberal arts program. My good friend Lala is now a teacher, my own sister is a social worker and a therapist, and many other Latino Baruch graduates have jobs as teachers, social workers, writers, and lawyers, including myself. We are all First-Generation Latinos who were able to take advantage of the opportunities made possible by our families' sacrifices. The common thread was that we all had expectations, as well as family to lean on. Unfortunately, many young Latinos do not have that kind of family support or are influenced negatively by their neighborhoods or environment. I believe that the trick is intervention, and to help these kids before it is too late. Unfortunately, funding for dropout prevention or other programs to help young inner-city kids is not prioritized and never has been in this country. In contrast, recent figures reveal that the annual cost for just one prison inmate in New York state was $69,355 in 2020 (and in NYC it was as high as $447,337). The total cost for state and federal inmates in the United States was over $50 billion as of 2020, with the annual cost per inmate being highest in the state of New York. Unfortunately, these numbers are swept under the rug and ignored due to powerful lobbyist groups and self-interested political agendas.

College was different from high school in many ways: there were no long school days like the usual eight to three, most classes were only one or two hours long, and students usually had two classes a day with one day off during the week. There was a lot of free time and students were treated like adults. It is frustrating to think about the numerous Latino kids who dropped out of school after being treated unfairly by teachers or school counselors that could not recognize or see their potential. These dropouts were missing out on opportunities for higher learning due to lowered expectations, misconceived notions or buying into stereotypes. Despite all the expectations and opportunities that a college education provided, students still had time for entertainment. Baruch did not have the traditional fraternities with house parties or keggers, but there were plenty of opportunities to have fun. During my freshman year, I found out that during "club hours" on Tuesdays and Thursdays, when students were given two hours to pursue extracurricular activities, some of the students were going to a local bar.

The Treaty Stone was a traditional Irish dive bar located on 3rd Avenue between 23rd and 24th Streets. I made my way over there as an eighteen-year-old freshman, and I fit right in. The drinking age was twenty-one, but at the Treaty Stone no one asked for ID. The bartender, Tommy, asked me on my first visit how old I was and of course I lied and told him I was twenty-one. Even though I looked like a baby and there is no way that anyone in their right mind would think I was twenty-one years old, Tommy looked at me, winked and asked, "What do you want?"

I always ordered rum and coke. I found out later that if you add lime to the rum and coke it is called a Cuba Libre. During the Spanish-American War, when Cuba was liberated from Spanish rule, a toast was made by Teddy Roosevelt's Rough Riders while drinking Cuban rum. "*Cuba libre!*" they shouted, which translates to "Free Cuba!" Cuba Libre sounds exotic and much better than just plain old rum and coke. They called my favorite bartender at the Treaty Stone "Tommy behind the bar." Never in a million years would I ever think that Tommy behind the bar would one day change my life forever!

The Treaty Stone was a classic New York City dive bar, which means that it had been around forever and the bar where drinks were served was made of old wood that smelled like a million drinks had been spilled on it over the years. The floors were sticky, and the bar always smelled like a mixture of alcohol and ammonia. I suppose the bar would be cleaned thoroughly with ammonia in the mornings after a full day of drinks being spilled and drunk patrons throwing up late at night after one too many. The bathrooms were unique as well since the urinals had ice cubes and ice chips in them. If the customers were too drunk or lazy to flush, the ice would take care of it. Sometimes it was fun when taking a leak to aim directly on the ice cubes and chips and watch them melt. There were also old cloth towel dispensers in the bathroom attached to the wall, and when you pulled on the towel a new section of towel would come out. I am not sure how long that towel was or whether the towels were cleaned or replaced, but I usually let my hands air dry after using the bathroom at the Treaty Stone. Most of the regular customers were old retired Irish men and barflies, but there were also some construction workers and civil service workers, like postal delivery workers in their uniforms and even police officers. The New York City police academy was only a few blocks away. Back then no one cared or enforced the law when it came to underage drinking. When I was going there, a group of students from Baruch would always be present during club hours.

Tommy and I became friends over the years. He told me that on the weekends he worked at a bar called Hickey's near Penn Station in the city. He said that I could stop by whenever I wanted, and he would hook me up. He also told me, "Don't bring your knucklehead college friends." He smiled and winked when he said that, so I guess he was kidding.

September 6, 1992, was an important date for me. It was the first weekend of the NFL football season. I was single and a sports fanatic, looking forward to pigging out on junk food and watching the Jets get their butts kicked, in the comfort of my own bedroom. My boy Joey called me that morning and reminded me that there was a Spanish music festival called El Fieston where we could meet pretty Latina girls. I was tired of these festivals. My dating life as a college student was pitiful, consisting of one-night stands and unfulfilling short-term relationships. The pretty girls that I chased, including some models and actresses, turned me down because I was a penniless college student. (I wasn't chasing anybody famous, of course, like the movie stars in LA; in New York there are many aspiring models and actresses that work as bartenders, waitresses and hostesses.) The girls who were interested in me were not my type. It was hard for me to be mean to anyone, so I told a lot of these girls that we could be friends. I did not want to go out because I was frustrated with my love life, but my boy Joey talked me into it. Joey was a music producer and he lived in Sound View in the Boogey Down, in the Bronx. He was friendly with Fat Joe, the most famous Latino rapper from the South Bronx. He was my partner in crime, and we met many women as we were trying to be "players" over the years, but at the end of the day, I just wanted to meet a nice girl. I was tired of the whole fly-by-night dating scene.

I met Pete in the city that day and it was the usual routine. He bragged about being a music producer and handed out business cards (he was a producer on the cult classic freestyle hit "Crying over You" by Suave). His company was called 40 Crew Productions, with the forty representing a forty-ounce beer. Back then it was hip to drink a forty, usually Old English Malt Liquor, known as Old E and Old Gold, or the other popular brand, Ballantine Ale. My liver cringes just thinking about all that cheap malt liquor we used to drink. All day long I talked to an endless number of women with whom I had nothing in common, but they were cute, so that was the point. However, back in the day, there were no iPhones and the numbers that these girls gave me were written on bubble gum wrappers that I had stuffed in my pocket. I could have brought a notepad, but if I wrote phone numbers in a notepad, the girls would think I was a player. So, I chewed a couple packs of gum throughout the day and kept the wrappers for the numbers. At this Spanish music festival, I don't even remember what bands were playing or what else was going on, we just went out like soldiers hunting for women. Today, in our woke world, it sounds misogynistic and pathetic, but that's just the way things were back in the day. Even so, I was never mean to any woman, and I truly enjoyed their company. I grew up with women my entire life and it was easier for me to talk to women than men. To this day, I prefer talking to women rather than men.

  At the end of the festival, I said my goodbyes to Joey and his boys and it was time to go home. The sun was setting, and I was tired and broke. I was headed toward Penn Station to take the Long Island Railroad home. I would take the Port Washington Line to Bayside because that was the fastest way home from the city. I was usually one of the only Latinos on the Port Washington Line train whenever I took the Long Island Railroad. If I did not take the railroad, I would have to take two subway trains and a bus and instead of a one-hour commute, it would be two hours. The only issue was that the railroad was much more expensive. Since it was late on a Sunday night and I was tired, I decided to take the railroad anyway because I had school the next day. After a long day of talking to girls and drinking, I was dying to use the bathroom. At New York City public events, the porta potties that are put out for the public are disgustingly dirty and have a horrible smell. I would rather hold it in than use one of those awful portable bathrooms. My saving grace was that only one block from Penn Station there was a dive bar called Hickey's and I knew Tommy from behind the bar would be working that night. I could go to Hickey's, use the bathroom, and then hang out with Tommy for a little while and get free drinks because I would tell him that I was broke and I would get him the next time. We were old friends from my early Baruch College days, and he knew I was good for it.

    I walked into Hickeys and the bar was empty. It was a Sunday night, after all. I immediately saw Tommy and I told him I wanted to use the bathroom. He said, "Of course, Ed, you know where it is." I went to the bathroom in the back of the bar, and it felt so good, as I had been holding it in for too long. I melted all the ice cubes in the urinal and then I washed my hands and let them air dry, ignoring the cloth towel dispenser. As I walked back to the bar from the bathroom, I noticed three girls sitting at the end of the bar near the entrance. I did not see them when I walked in because I was in such a rush to use the bathroom and I went straight to the back. Tommy had a rum and coke waiting for me at the bar; I didn't even have to ask. I loved Tommy, my favorite bartender of all time! I sat down and I explained to him that I was broke, and he said, "No worries, it's on the house."

    As I sat there, I noticed that those girls were having fun and were laughing and joking around. One of those girls looked young and it turns out that she was Tommy's niece. Another looked older and worn, like she had been through some things. The third one was young and pretty with beautiful long hair and she looked like someone I would like to get to know. She was wearing a T-shirt and jeans and had no makeup on, but she had that natural look. She was slim and looked athletic, but more importantly she had a pretty face. Where had she been all day while I was walking around everywhere at that Spanish festival? They were at the end of the bar, and I was planning to head over there at the right moment. I was a little shocked that a sweet-looking, pretty girl like her would be at a dive bar like Hickey's, but it was New York City after all, and nothing should really shock anyone in New York City.

I later found out that the cute girl with the natural beauty was Sandy Lanza, a First-Generation Latina girl who grew up in an inner-city neighborhood, Long Island City and was a student at Baruch College. Her parents were from Honduras. She loved salsa music and wanted to go to the El Fieston salsa festival to see some of her favorite bands and singers. Her older sister Claudia, who was a recovering drug addict and alcoholic, had recently moved back in with the family after another failed relationship. Claudia tagged along with her sister that day to go to El Fieston. Sandy was so excited that she bought a new camera for the occasion and brought it with her to take pictures of some of her favorite salsa singers. When they arrived at El Fieston, Claudia was already drunk and was buying beer from street vendors left and right. Sandy asked her sister to carry the camera case so that she could take pictures throughout the day. In the early afternoon, Claudia was bugging Sandy because she had to go to the bathroom after drinking so much beer. At this point, poor Sandy was babysitting her sister. Claudia abruptly walked into the nearest bar, which was Hickey's. Sandy yelled at Claudia because she would never be caught dead in a place like that. Claudia just stormed in, and Sandy had to follow her sister. After

Claudia used the bathroom, of course she stayed to have a drink despite Sandy's complaining.

They met the Hickey's bartender, Tommy. After a few drinks, Sandy made Claudia leave because she knew her sister would want to stay there all afternoon. Sandy was there to see the salsa bands and singers at El Fieston, not to get wasted at a dive bar. Claudia had only one job that day: to hold onto the camera case. Of course, she couldn't even get that right and she left the camera case at the bar. When the festival was over, Sandy asked Claudia for the camera case. Claudia was drunk and started crying. "I'm sorry, I lost the case." Sandy was livid! The camera was expensive, and she had worked long hours at her part-time job to save up for it. While Claudia was blubbering incoherently, Sandy thought that perhaps Claudia had left the case at Hickey's bar. They went back to Hickey's and Sandy was furious because she did not want to go to that nasty dive bar again. When they walked into the bar, Tommy the bartender said, "Hey ladies, did you forget something?" He was holding the case in his hands. Tommy's niece had stopped by to visit her uncle and she asked Sandy and Claudia to stay and have a few drinks with her. Tommy said the drinks were on the house – he was cool that way – and Sandy finally gave in and decided to stay.

As I sat at the other end of the bar waiting to make my move, I heard someone yell from across the bar "Hey you, you go to Baruch?"

I said yes, and then Sandy's sister Claudia yelled, "Get over here!"

How could these girls know that I went to Baruch? Then it dawned on me I was wearing my lucky Baruch basketball jersey underneath my jacket. When I went over there, I immediately realized that Sandy was shy, and her sister had called to me on her behalf. Sandy and I immediately clicked. I could actually talk to her about all kinds of things, and I could tell that she was smart. She mentioned more than once that she had been going to Baruch for four years and that she had a 3.9 GPA in accounting. I was very impressed, and I immediately realized that she was marriage material. I was not looking to settle down, but I knew that this was a quality girl. As I talked to Sandy, I forgot that anyone else was there.

After a few drinks it was getting late, and I asked Sandy for her phone number. She had a little notepad and wrote her number on a sheet of paper that looked like graph paper. She then asked me for my wallet and folded it in four and neatly put it into my wallet. Strangely enough, by the time I got home I was so tired and drunk that I had somehow lost all those phone numbers I had written on bubble gum wrappers. Sandy was smart to put her phone number in my wallet. Sandy and I had been going to Baruch at the same time and I had never seen her there. We finally met at a dive bar in New York City! Hickey's finally went out of business a few years later and the building became a trendy bar/lounge where the drinks are overpriced and the customers try to act hip or brag about being wealthy. Unfortunately, I also found out that Tommy passed away. I will never forget Tommy behind the bar.

After that night I waited two weeks to call Sandy. I was still talking to a few girls, and I was still single after all. I was a cardio workout warrior, and I was very fit. I didn't want to seem desperate or overanxious but, in retrospect, perhaps two weeks was too long. Nevertheless, when I called her, we spoke for hours. I lost track of the time and can't remember exactly what we talked about, but I remember having a warm feeling in my stomach the whole time. We agreed to go out on a Saturday night, and I would pick her up at her apartment in Long Island City. I was going to take her to a club called the Melting Pot because I had passes to get in, and back then every penny counted because I was always broke. I told Sandy that I knew where she lived because I actually believed that was true. Keep in mind this was before GPS or Map Quest. On the night of our first date, I left my house early because I wanted to make a good first impression. I would pick her up in my suburban limousine, my dad's maroon Caprice Classic station wagon since I did not have my own car. Unfortunately, I did not know where Sandy lived, even though I thought I did. I was driving all over Astoria and she lived in Long Island City. I was determined to find her apartment without calling her for directions because I wanted to make a good impression. After driving around for what seemed like forever, I stopped at an Irish bar for directions. I bought a drink to be polite and the bartender gave me directions. It turns out I was only a few blocks away from Sandy's apartment. Then when I looked at the time, I realized that I was two hours late.

When I finally got to Sandy's place, she was standing outside of her apartment building with her sister, Claudia. She told me that she thought I was going to stand her up. I was so embarrassed, and I apologized and pleaded my case, just short of crying. Then when I took a good look at Sandy, I did not recognize her. She had proofed out her hair, kind of like Sandy at the end of the movie *Grease*. She was wearing makeup and a sexy top with tight, form-fitting Edwin jeans (seriously, that was a popular brand back in the day), and knee-high, sexy leather boots. She was very curvaceous and had a nice body. I was smitten and shocked that she looked so hot and so different from the girl I met at the bar. Soon we were off to the city in my dad's station wagon. She never complained about the car, and it seemed like she forgave me for being late. We met my friend James and some of his friends at a bar. The drinks at the Melting Pot were expensive, so we bought cheap drinks at the bar before going to the club, which, oddly enough, was only a few blocks away from Baruch. We went to the club and danced all night. I loved dancing freestyle and club music, and she liked my moves. It was not a traditional first date, but it was perfect for us. During the night I got quite sweaty and hot, so I asked her if she would mind if I opened my shirt while on the dance floor. She said no, so I opened my shirt, and she was able to see my washboard abs. I seriously did not do it on purpose, but I worked out a lot back then. I took her home that night and gave her a kiss on the cheek goodbye. I called her the next day as soon as I woke up. I knew that I was going to marry that girl one day!

Sandy and I started dating and even took a class together at Baruch. It was cool to take a college class with my girlfriend because we could kiss before and after class. I was so in love that I wrote her poems and gave her love letters before class. We would go out to eat after class and it was like a date every time. The class we took together was an advanced Spanish class, as an elective. Obviously, we sat together and my friend Jasmine also took the class and sat nearby. During the final exam, Jasmine was copying Sandy's answers, and they were caught by Professor Quintian. In front of the whole class, he told them that they were only cheating themselves. Sandy was extremely embarrassed, and I felt guilty because I had introduced Sandy to Jasmine. Sandy still gives me a hard time about this, but it was actually funny because the straight-A student had met me a short time ago and already was getting in trouble with a teacher for the first time in her life. In spite of that, Sandy and I both received A's in the class. At the end of the year, we graduated together, and it was really special: we were two inner-city First-Generation Latino kids whose parents came to the United States with no money to make a better life for their families. We were the first in our families to graduate from college. Our graduation would take place at the Theater at Madison Square Garden. Being Latino in New York City and graduating from Baruch, we thought the setting was perfect. I had been to so many New York Knick games over the years. The Garden was the Mecca where there had been so many concerts with famous bands and famous musicians like the Rolling Stones, Genesis, Billy Joel, Sting, Phil Collins, Mark Anthony, Ricky Martin, Hector Lavoe, and a host of others. Sandy and I heard our names called during the ceremony and we were able to accept our diplomas in the place where so many fans had seen their idols. I felt very proud! Our two families went to a Colombian restaurant in Jackson Heights to celebrate after the ceremony. It was a classic Latino celebration for two First-Generation New York City kids.

Even though I was a college graduate who lived in the suburbs, on Christmas Eve, 1994, I was rudely reminded that I was still a Latino living in New York City. That night I had plans to meet Sandy at her apartment in Long Island City to celebrate Christmas. She still lived with her family in an ethnic neighborhood in Queens. I went to the city that afternoon to get a haircut and do some shopping. Since it was the holidays and the owner of the barbershop was Greek, they were offering shots of a Greek liqueur called ouzo. I took a few shots because I was excited to be near my alma mater and to have plans to see my girlfriend later that evening. I decided to visit my old stomping grounds around Baruch College, and I stopped at the old Treaty Stone, now called Openers, to have a drink. One of my old friends was at the bar and bought me a few rounds and we did some shots of tequila. Back then I weighed about 150 pounds, and I was drinking more than my body could assimilate. I did not intend to drink so much, and I certainly did not want to go to Sandy's house drunk.

I decided to take a cab to her apartment because it was a short ride from the bar to Long Island City. I asked the cab driver to drop me off a few blocks from her apartment because I wanted to get breath mints and grab a snack at a nearby bodega. I forgot that Sandy had told me that drugs were sold at that bodega, and it was a dangerous place. I walked in and it was crowded. I talked to a few people in front of and behind the counter in Spanish, and as I recall we were joking around. I don't remember anything after that. I found out later that one or more New York City police officers beat the hell out of me. I was the Latino version of Rodney King without the publicity. They claim that I threw myself against parking meters and the sidewalk. I would never do that to myself. I was knocked unconscious, so I will never truly know what happened to me that night. Perhaps I was belligerent because the police violated my rights without cause. Maybe I cursed at one of the officers for touching me or questioning me. I believe they only saw me as lowlife Latino trash!

Somebody called Sandy from a phone number I had on me. I was only a few blocks away from her house. Poor Sandy came running out in her pajamas and a winter coat as soon as she got the call. When she arrived at the scene, one of the officers asked her, "What was your boyfriend doing in this neighborhood, at that deli, at that hour?"

I was a bloody mess and was being put into an ambulance. I ask myself today, once it is established that someone is clearly not a threat, why beat them to a pulp or try to kill them? When I woke up, I was in a hospital gown on a gurney, Sandy and my family were praying for me and my Abuelita Hortencia was crying. Everyone was relieved when I came to, but I was angry and ashamed. The police denied any wrongdoing and supposedly no one at the deli remembered seeing anything. It was a big cover-up and after my wounds healed, I managed to let it go, but I will never forget!

I was idealistic, so after I graduated from Baruch College with a Bachelor of Arts in psychology, I wanted to try to change the world. I wanted to help inner-city kids and make a real difference for minority kids. It was the mid-90s, and I was able to get my dream job as a counselor in a tough Brooklyn school, John Jay High School. The students were predominantly Black and Latino from inner-city neighborhoods, including Bedford-Stuyvesant, Bushwick, Red Hook, Sunset Park, and East Flatbush. I was working for Good Shepherd Services in a dropout prevention and college prep program for at-risk kids. We helped anyone who wanted help but recruited at-risk kids. I worked with gang members, outcasts, kids that felt alienated and kids that were struggling academically. We worked with young students to give them goals and options for the future.

Intervention was the key. At that time, John Jay High School had over twenty gangs represented in the school. There were many sad and frustrating stories that still haunt me today. One of the students that I counseled was shot and killed over a girl and a turf issue. There was an unfortunate Arabic girl who was an honor student and wanted to go to college and medical school, but her parents made her get married and move to the Middle East at a young age. There was a smart and charismatic gang member who could have accomplished anything that he chose to do, but he decided to drop out of school. I spent countless hours advising him that he had the potential to do whatever he wanted. His choice was to be a leader of a Latin Kings set with hundreds of members. So many sad stories and I wish I could have done more.

I was frustrated by the senseless violence as well as a lack of resources and an apathetic school administration. There was a waiting list for a day-care program because teen pregnancy was so prevalent. Young female students would come to school early to drop off their babies before they would go to class. When classes started at the beginning of the semester there were not enough seats for all the students. However, after a few weeks, the classes were half-empty due to truancy or a lack of interest. There were not enough textbooks to go around so kids were not allowed to take them home. We provided a safe haven for students and offered tutoring and mentoring programs at the Good Shepherd offices located in the school. We made overnight and weekend trips to colleges to open these kids' eyes and give them hope. We helped a lot of kids and many of them went to college. I enjoyed my time at John Jay, but I was only making eleven dollars an hour, and my girlfriend Sandy wanted to get married and buy a house. These programs should have been overly funded rather than struggling to stay afloat. I will always cherish my time at John Jay High School.

With a heavy heart, I left my dream job and applied to law school. I was accepted to St. John's School of law and because of my work with Good Shepherd Services, my volunteer work, my involvement with minority youths and my own background. I received a merit scholarship. I also received a small scholarship from the Latin American and Black studies department at Baruch College, which meant the world to me. My mentor, Professor Wilson, nominated me and I was very proud when I won. Law school was expensive, and my scholarships only covered a third of my costs, but the scholarships did help and I was very grateful for them. My mother, who was my biggest fan and never gave up on me despite my struggles, cried when she found out I was accepted to law school. She was still struggling with lymphoma and her health was deteriorating, but I believe that I gave her the strength to live a few more years.

I married my girlfriend Sandy, and she supported me through law school. She grew up the same way that I did, and I was proud of her when she graduated Magna Cum Laude with an accounting degree from Baruch. She got a job as an accountant at Con Edison and encouraged me to go to law school. She will forever be the love of my life. Early on, we lived in my parents' basement, and she was very understanding. We had a modest but beautiful wedding. My sister, Valeria, who was eighteen years old at the time, had a baby. My little niece, Tatiana, also gave my mother the strength to live a few more years.

During my third and last year of law school, my mother's B-cell lymphoma morphed into a more aggressive T-cell lymphoma. I spoke to her oncologist at length and the prognosis was bleak: my mother only had months to live. My mother told me not to get distracted and to keep studying hard. Soon I would have to take the bar exam, which is considered one of the hardest professional exams in the world. My mother's illness gave me a drive that I had never felt in my life until then. There was no way that I would let her down. As my mother received aggressive chemotherapy and radiation treatments, I studied so hard that I thought my eyes would roll out of my head. My mother was so sick she could not even attend my graduation ceremony, but as soon as it was over, I kept my cap and gown on and rushed home to hug and kiss her. I cried and held her as hard as I could.

"Mami, because you never gave up on me, look what I have accomplished." We both cried until she felt so weak that she had to lie down. I took the bar exam and even though it was stressful, I thought it was easy. My mother gave me so much encouragement to overcome any obstacles and because of her, I was as well prepared as anyone taking that exam. Once the exam was over, I could dedicate all my time to my dying mother.

During the entire summer of 2000, I took my mother to all of her chemotherapy and radiation appointments. My beautiful mother lost all of her hair and looked gaunt and frail, but in my mind, she still was the vibrant, lovely woman I had always known. We spent hours talking to each other and I apologized for my rebellious teen years and begged her to forgive me for not being a better son. Why was God doing this to me and why did I waste so many years underappreciating my dear mother? She was so sick and weak, and I catered to her every need; whenever she had a craving for anything, I would get it. Half of the time she could not hold anything down, but if she asked for it, I got it. She often asked for *parbo rojo* (red snapper) Colombian style and *maduros* (sweet plantains). At a local health food store, I found some food that her stomach could tolerate.

I would not start working until the fall, so I had the whole summer to spend time with her. I would begin working as a Criminal Prosecutor in Brooklyn for the New York City Law Department in September. It was a blessing to spend the summer with my mother, but it hurt my heart to see her suffer. We were hopeful that the aggressive treatment could turn the tide, but I was always inquisitive, so I spoke to the doctors at length and the prognosis was dire. She was referred for an experimental clinical chemotherapy trial in Fresh Meadows, Queens. My mother was fighting for her life and, as a family, we decided that it was worth it.

In an eerie twist of fate, the facility for this experimental treatment was near a private Catholic cemetery. I would have to drive by the cemetery every time I took her for treatment. One day she told me that if she died, she wanted to be buried there. "No, Mami, don't say that" I protested, but she was very pragmatic. Deep down I knew that this was a harsh reality that we had to face.

Shortly before I started working, my mother told me that she did not feel well, and she wanted to go to the hospital. All summer we had cared for her at home, while she had lost her hair, fainted, and vomited, so for her to say that she wanted to go to the hospital meant that it was urgent. I drove her to the Flushing Hospital of Queens and parked my dad's car in front of the hospital even though I knew I would get a ticket. My poor mother looked scared, and she could barely walk, so I had to carry her into the hospital. There were no cell phones back then so I could not call the family at that moment. Her oncologist was affiliated with the hospital, so my mother was admitted, and she never came home after that day. During that first week, she started bleeding profusely through every orifice: nose, ears, mouth, etc. When the nurses could not keep up with the job, my wife, Sandy, would clean and care for her. That's when I knew that she was going to be my wife forever. It got to the point that she needed blood transfusions to stay alive. Her doctor asked us if we would just let her bleed out; without a blood transfusion, she would die and not suffer anymore. I don't know whether we made the right or wrong decision, but I could not let my mother just die if there was something that the doctors could do.

My mother suffered for a few more weeks, but the family was always with her and selfishly I am glad that she was able to say goodbye to me and everyone else and make her peace with God. Toward the end she looked happy and calm. I started working and all I could do was wait until my workday was over so that I could rush to the hospital. The day before she died, she called me and asked me to talk to her doctors. She felt like it was almost time to go but wanted to be sure. I was outside of the Brooklyn Court House on Adams Street, and I cried hysterically. I have no clue what all the lawyers and pedestrians passing by must have thought, but I felt like it was just me, my mother and God in the street at that moment.

The next morning, I went to work. I got to my office in Brooklyn and my supervisor told me that she wanted to talk to me. Someone had called the office and told her that my mother had passed away that morning. I was angry at first because selfishly I wished I could have been there with her, holding her hand when she died. I immediately rushed to the hospital, but with the New York City subway and bus delays working against me, it took over an hour to get there. When at last I arrived, she was being put in a body bag, a long black bag like a giant garbage bag, and someone was closing a zipper on her. My wife and family were there but I did not see anything but that zipper closing and my poor mami's lifeless body. I was dressed for work, wearing my suit and tie, but I immediately jumped on top of her lifeless body, and the man that was closing the bag knew that he needed to step away. I lay on top of her and kissed her and hugged her for what seemed like an eternity. It took my entire family to pull me off my mother. Our family was never the same. My mother will always be a part of me, and I will never forget her. I have mourned for twenty years but we are building a new family bond.

Exactly what does Second-Generation mean? It means that my daughters Christina and Liliana and my niece Tatiana had parents that were born and raised in the United States. It means that they did not have to grow up wearing hand-me-down clothing, they did not have to witness atrocities such as muggings, rapes and murders committed on a daily basis in the neighborhoods where they were being raised. It means that they did not have to grow up in a roach- and rat-infested apartment, they did not have to worry about stray bullets during gunfights between gang members and shootouts between criminals and the police. It means that they did not have to hide the fact that they were Latinas in order to assimilate, fit in or face overt racism on a daily basis. All of the abuelitos and abuelitas who came to this country looking for better opportunities can now admire the rewards of their sacrifices, either here on this earth or from up above in heaven. They had children in the United States who succeeded as American citizens and those children had children.

This second wave of Latinos are prospering today! We now have Second-Generation Latino politicians, CEOs of Fortune five hundred companies and countless famous actors and singers who do not have to change their surnames to appeal to mainstream America. I am proud to say that today Latinos wear their ethnicity and heritage as a badge of honor. We are the fastest-growing population in the United States. Thanks to my immigrant parents' sacrifices and Sandy's and my ability to guide our children through all the pitfalls associated with growing up Latino in New York City and our setting a good example as educated Latino professionals, they do not have any limits on what they can achieve, and they can dare to aim high.

My twelve-year-old daughter Liliana was the first female Latino student to be elected president at her junior high school.

She was also invited to attend the Junior National Young Leaders Conference in Washington DC. I am proud to say that she gave the commencement speech at her graduation. As a trial attorney and public speaker, I was able to help her with her speech, so she reaped the benefits of being a Second-Generation Latina. She did an excellent job and received a standing ovation. I can honestly say that her presentation was as good as or better than many of the briefs delivered by the trial lawyers I go up against in court.

My sixteen-year-old daughter Christina is a junior in high school and is being recruited by over a hundred colleges. She is on the principal's list and is vying for valedictorian of her high school. She was elected to be part of the National Honor Society and serves as the vice president of the Language Honors Society.

It is important to note that I have never laid a finger on my children, as I vowed to break the vicious cycle of corporal punishment practiced by many immigrant parents. More importantly, I have never pushed them to overachieve. My niece Tatiana, who is a twenty-five-year-old Second-Generation Latina, was able to graduate from college Summa cum Laude with a scholarship and then received her master's degree in school counseling. She is currently a counselor at a prestigious high school in Long Island, New York. The common thread is that the second generation does not have to dream, they can actually have goals that can be realized. They have parents who can guide them realistically toward higher education, support them in any endeavors that they choose to pursue, and encourage them to achieve anything for which they have a passion.

The second generation gives the Latin X community hope and the future looks bright.

Printed in the USA
CPSIA information can be obtained
at www.ICGtesting.com
LVHW091329290324
775820LV00001B/9